The Orthodox Pastor

A Guide to Pastoral Theology

Second Edition

ARCHBISHOP
JOHN SHAHOVSKOY

ST VLADIMIR'S SEMINARY PRESS
Crestwood, New York
2008

Library of Congress Cataloging-in-Publication Data

Ioann, Archbishop of San Francisco and Western United States, 1902–1989.
  The Orthodox pastor : a guide to pastoral theology / John Shahovskoy.
— 2nd ed.
      p.   cm.
    ISBN 978–0–913836–03–3 (alk. paper)
   1. Pastoral theology—Orthodox Eastern Church.   I. Title.
    BX341.6.I5313 2008
    262'.1419—dc22

                                                    2007050728

Published in Russian as
List'ia Dreva: Opyt Pravoslavnogo Dukhovedeniia
(Leaves of the Tree: An Experience of Orthodox Pastorship)

First English Edition 1966
Foreword to Second Edition Copyright © 2008
ST VLADIMIR'S SEMINARY PRESS
575 Scarsdale Rd, Crestwood, NY 10707
1-800-204-2665
www.svspress.com

ISBN 978–0–913836–03–3

Contents

Contents continued

PART TWO

Foreword to Second Edition

THE PRESENT modest book by Archbishop John (Shahovskoy) first appeared in English in 1966, as one of the very first publications of St. Vladimir's Seminary Press. It was not selected for translation and publication because it was new or "cutting edge." As Fr. Alexander Schmemann notes in his Foreword to the first edition, the book had appeared in the Russian language many decades before. It was selected because it distilled the wisdom and insights of one of the finest pastors and spiritual writers of the Russian emigration.

The future Archbishop John was born in Moscow in 1902, as Prince Dimitry Shahovskoy. In the wake of the Russian Revolution and civil war, he made his way first to Belgium and France, where he gained distinction as a poet and essayist, and then to Mount Athos, where he was tonsured as a monk in 1926. Thereafter, as a young hieromonk, he pursued an energetic pastoral and educational ministry in Yugoslavia and Germany. As World War II swept over Europe, his ministry extended to the many Russian slave laborers and prisoners of war who were forced to work in the factories of Nazi Germany. Displaced again in the aftermath of the war, Fr. John came to the United States, where he was instrumental in organizing aid and sponsorship for other refugees and displaced persons. In 1947 he was consecrated as Bishop of Brooklyn and appointed Dean of St. Vladimir's Seminary, then in New York City. Around this time he also began his forty-year ministry as a religious broadcaster to the Soviet Union. In 1950 he was elected as Bishop of San Francisco, being elevated to the rank of archbishop in 1961. Although he retired from active ministry in 1979, Archbishop John continued to be involved in the literary and cultural life of San Francisco's Russian community until his death in 1989.

3

In the same year that Archbishop John took up his episcopal responsibilities in San Francisco, my future wife and her family, the Manturoffs, immigrated to the United States from China, and as dedicated members of San Francisco's Holy Trinity Cathedral parish, they entered actively into church life. Archbishop John became their archpastor and friend. In time he was instrumental in my own introduction into the Manturoff family, and in 1964, in connection with what eventually came to be known as "Orthodox Education Day," he ordained me to the Holy Priesthood in the old chapel of St. Vladimir's Seminary. These divinely guided and grace-empowered occurrences, in a deeply personal way, link me with Archbishop John forever. They have been a source of joy, inspiration, and gratitude throughout my own pastoral ministry.

Although *The Orthodox Pastor* is not a new book, by republishing it St. Vladimir's Seminary Press underscores the fact that its content never grows old. Certainly, in the course of my own ministry, I have turned to it again and again for inspiration and sage counsel. Authored by an experienced and Spirit-bearing mentor, the book continues to stand out, in all its aspects, as a foundational guide toward the concrete realization, within the ordained ministry of the Orthodox Church in any land or age, of the never-ending pastorship of our Lord and Savior Jesus Christ—the Good Shepherd and High Priest, who, making "all things new" (Rev 21:5), is "the same, yesterday, and today and forever" (Heb 13:8).

—THE VERY REV. PAUL LAZOR
John and Paraskeva Skvir Lecturer in Pastoral Theology
and Associate Dean for Student Affairs (retired)
St. Vladimir's Orthodox Theological Seminary

It is a great honor and also a great joy for us at St. Vladimir's Seminary to publish this *Outline of Pastoral Theology* by our former Dean, His Grace, Archbishop John of San Francisco. He is one of the great spiritual writers of our time and it is indeed unfortunate that virtually none of his writings have as yet appeared in English. For they contain that which we need more than anything else in our confused era: the testimony of a spiritual experience rooted in a spiritual reality.

This book was published in Russian more than thirty years ago and reflects a pastoral situation in many ways different from the one we face today here in America. But the pastoral work, dependent as it is on ever-changing "situations" and "cultures," remains essentially the same in all of them, for its only real object is the human soul and its eternal destiny. It is of this unchanging essence of priesthood and ministry that Archbishop John writes here and his message is especially timely now— when even the Church seems to be tempted so often by a human, external and material idea of "success." A careful reader will no doubt discern how to apply it to his practical needs.

Forty years have elapsed since Archbishop John took his monastic vows on Mount Athos and twenty since his episcopal consecration in New York. On this double anniversary let this book be the token of our gratitude to a spiritual teacher who has truly taught us—by his life and by his writings—to seek the "one thing needful" (LUKE 10, 42).

— THE VERY REV. ALEXANDER SCHMEMANN,
Dean, St. Vladimir's Seminary

5

INTRODUCTION

1

The One Pastorship

THERE IS NOTHING more awe-inspiring and more blessed than the service of pastorship.

Through earthly and heavenly shepherds the Lord feeds His flock of the believing, or of the not yet believing, souls.

True pastorship is Christ's life continuing in the world. "Thou art a priest for ever after the order of Melchisedec."

However many shepherds there may be on earth or in heaven, there always remains One Unchangeable Shepherd. However many churches there may be in the world, there always remains One Orthodox Church, rightly-glorifying Christ and free from all frailty or defilement.

Only those who know the One Shepherd can be shepherds on earth or in heaven.

"The Lord is my shepherd; I shall not want. He maketh me to lie down in green pastures; He leadeth me beside the still waters. He restoreth my soul; He leadeth me in the paths of righteousness for His name's sake. Yea, though I walk through the valley of the shadow of death, I will fear no evil; for Thou art with me..." (Ps. 23).

"He will feed His flock as a shepherd; He shall gather the lambs with His arm, and carry them in His bosom, and shall gently lead those that are with young" (Is. 40, 11).

"Behold, I, even I, will both search my sheep and seek them out. As a shepherd seeketh out his flock in the day that he is among his sheep that are scattered; so will I seek out my sheep, and will deliver them out of all places where they have been scattered in the cloudy and dark day. . . . I will feed them in good pasture, and upon the high mountains of Israel shall their fold be; there shall they lie in a good fold, and in a fat pasture shall they feed upon the mountains of Israel. I will feed my flock, and I will cause them to lie down, saith the Lord God. I will seek that which was lost, and bring again that which was driven away, and will bind up that which was broken, and will strengthen that which was sick: but I will destroy the fat and the strong; I will feed them with judgment" (EZEKIEL 34, 11-16).

Everyone who has done pastoral work knows what a joy it is to find believers lost in the world but preserved by the Shepherds' hand. One meets such souls at different cross-roads in life and in the stillness of complete solitude. It would seem that no one had ever approached them, no one had ever attempted spiritually to captivate them, no earthly pastor had ever come near them with a view to their salvation and that they had never heard a word of spiritual encouragement from anyone. And yet they spiritually grow and flourish; the path of faith becomes clearer to them and the true ways of life grow more distinct.

Sometimes these people receive no help whatever from others all their life, and indeed everything round them seems to hinder them, to tempt and lead them astray. . . . And yet they flourish all the same and do not go astray, but shine with a heavenly light in the darkness around them.

Sometimes worse things happen: earthly pastors and masters who should sustain and comfort the soul push it away from the gracious light and teach it by their words or the example of their life something other than what the Lord Jesus Christ has taught us. This temptation often begins in early childhood, when a child does not see the Light of Christ in its home. But the Lord leads the soul which *consents* to this inner, heavenly guidance. And if the soul does consent to this inner, subtle guidance of conscience, to this perpetual burning of the heart which strives for light, suffers from darkness and repulses it— nothing can pluck it out of the Lord's hand. The words come true: "My sheep hear my voice (speaking in the depths of the heart and calling it to the heavenly light) and I know them, and they follow me . . . neither shall any man pluck them out of my hand" (JOHN 10, 27-28). Only those can be pastors and lead men to eternal life who themselves know the Shepherd and *whom the Shepherd knows*: "I am the good shepherd, and know my sheep, and am known of mine. . ." (JOHN 10, 14). This is the first condition of pastorship.

"It is written in the prophets: and they shall all be taught of God. Every man therefore that hath heard, and hath learned of the Father, cometh unto me" (JOHN 6, 65).

"The God of peace brought again from the dead our Lord Jesus, that great Shepherd of the sheep, through the blood of the everlasting covenant" (HEBR. 13, 20).

If it has seemed, and often still seems, that people on earth have no Shepherd ("they were like sheep without a shepherd. . ."), that means that the Shepherd who stands near these people is either unnoticed or repulsed by them. *But He remains their Shepherd all the same.*

9

Just as the Lord is the Saviour of all men, especially of those that believe (TIM. 4, 10), so He is the Shepherd of all mankind, especially of the faithful, i.e. of those who listen to Him, trust Him and follow Him.

"My sheep hear my voice, and I know them, and *they follow me. . . .*" Such is the relation between the Shepherd and the sheep of His flock, of His fold.

There are sheep *not of His fold,* and there are sheep of *another* fold of His: "other sheep I have, which are not of this fold: them also I must bring, and they shall hear my voice; and there shall be one fold and one Shepherd" (JOHN 10, 16). There are sheep who do not as yet follow their Shepherd, do not as yet belong to His visible fold, but they are His all the same. What a comfort this is to those who are troubled about the fate of nations and individual souls not included in the humanly visible fold of the Church! And what a warning to those who are within that fold! The first *at present* are not of this fold (not Orthodox and perhaps not even Christian), but all who live according to conscience and in the spirit of Cornelius the centurion shall come to Him and sit down at His feet. But some who are of 'this fold'—the fold of the visible Apostolic Church—may be thrust out like the Pharisees (for spiritual pride) or like the Sadducees (for unbelief).

St. Augustine says that the earthly Church is like a net which is plunged into the sea. Not all the fish that are in it at the moment shall be brought ashore (to the Kingdom of God) and some fish which are not in the net as yet, shall be caught in it.

Not everyone who thinks that he is following the One Shepherd is really following Him; and not everyone who is not following is really not following. Such persecutors of Christ as Saul are closer to Him than such worshippers as Ananias and Sapphira (ACTS 5).

The True and Only Shepherd does not have respect of persons nor does He consider whether a person is or is not included by men in His flock. He has the book of life and He Himself writes men's names in it, and no one but He can read this book or even open it (REV. 5, 3-4).

2

Evil Pastorship

I<small>F</small> S<small>CRIBES AND</small> P<small>HARISEES</small> sat in Moses' seat, guarded by the wall of the Law (M<small>ATT.</small> 23, 2), they could sit all the more easily in the seat of the One Meek Shepherd and *wrongly administer* the word of His truth. This is what has happened in the world. Wolves have entered the Shepherd's flock and begun to scatter His sheep— and they do so this day, having established themselves in churches and nations.

Pseudo-pastorship is the cruellest scourge that wounds the Most Pure Body of Christ. No human sins are comparable to the sin of false pastorship.

The father of false pastors is the devil, according to Christ's words: "ye are of your father, the devil" (J<small>OHN</small> 8, 44).

If any man *have not the spirit of Christ,* the sweet savour of the Gospel and the fervour of the apostles *he is none of His* (R<small>OM.</small> 8, 9). And if a man is not Christ's, whose is he?

False pastors who do *their own will* (and not Christ's) and follow after their own passions and lusts are the scourge of the Church. It is difficult to struggle against them, for in tearing them out of the holy body of the Church, one wounds the body. But it is necessary to struggle against them—by prayer and action.

A particularly heavy responsibility rests on bishops who "lay hands suddenly" (I Tɪᴍ. 5, 22).

By the mouth of His prophets God utters fiery, terrible words against shepherds who do not feed His flock and do not serve the One Shepherd. The prophets describe not only the shepherds' complete indifference to their work but their positive criminality.

In a war the enemy tries most of all to gain possession of the army chiefs, to penetrate into the staff, to the governing bodies, and so through the treason of one man to do more damage to the opponents' ranks than through victory on the battlefield. And in the spiritual war the enemy of the Shepherd uses all his wiles to gain possession of the shepherds of the Church—in the first instance, of bishops, priests, readers, monks, then of teachers, writers, rulers of states, parents, tutors . . . and through them to paralyze the power of the Lord's Church and most effectively contrive men's perdition.

Through finding his way to the pulpit the enemy can produce more devastation in the flock than through fighting in the union of militant atheists or through the decrees of a godless government. His purpose is to disrupt *from within*. And so he steals up both to the shepherds who are sleeping and to those who are merely dozing and gains possession of their feelings, words and actions, giving them *his* spirit — the spirit which brings spiritual ruin to men, destroying their faith in the Holy.*

The enemy wants "the salt to lose its savour" (Mᴀᴛᴛ. 5, 13), the Christians to lose the spirit of God, the shepherds to lose the One Shepherd.

Two things are equally terrible in a priest: iniquity that strikes the eye and leads many into temptation, and

---

* This is why St. John Chrysostom wrote: "There is no one whom I fear more than the bishops—with the exception of a few" (From a letter to St. Olympias).

outwardly invisible indifference to Christ's work, luke-warmness (REV. 3, 16), owing to which a priest (imperceptibly even to himself) puts himself in God's place and worships *himself* instead of God. He carries out the letter of the pastoral office, without having its spirit, *without entering into the work performed in the world by the One Shepherd.*

"The priests said not, Where is the Lord ? and they that handle the law know me not: the pastors also transgressed against me" (JER. 2, 8)—this is how God's word describes the priests' indifference.

"The pastors are become brutish, and have not sought the Lord; therefore they shall not prosper, and all their flocks shall be scattered" (JER. 10, 21).

"Many pastors have destroyed my vineyard, they have trodden my portion under foot, they have made my pleasant portion a desolate wilderness. They have made it desolate, and being desolate it mourneth unto me; the whole land is made desolate, because no man layeth it to heart" (JER. 12, 10-11).

"Woe be unto the pastors that destroy and scatter the sheep of my pasture ! saith the Lord" (JER. 23, 1).

"Howl, ye shepherds, and cry; and wallow yourselves in the ashes, ye principal of the flock: for the days of your slaughter and of your dispersions are accomplished; and ye shall fall like a pleasant vessel. And the shepherds shall have no way to flee, nor the principal of the flock to escape" (JER. 25, 34-35).

"And the word of the Lord came unto me, saying, son a man, prophesy against the shepherds of Israel, prophesy and say unto them, thus says the Lord God unto the shepherds: Woe be to the shepherds of Israel that do feed themselves ! should not the shepherds feed the flock? Ye eat the fat, and ye clothe you with wool, ye kill them that are fed; but ye feed not the flock. The diseased have

14

you not strengthened, neither have ye healed that which was sick, neither have ye bound that which was broken, neither have ye brought again that which was driven away, neither have ye sought that which was lost; but with force and with cruelty have ye ruled them. And they were scattered, because there is no shepherd; and they became meat to all the beasts of the field when they were scattered. My sheep wandered through all the mountains, and upon every high hill: yea, my flock was scattered upon all the face of the earth, and none did search or seek after them. Therefore, ye shepherds, hear the word of the Lord: As I live, saith the Lord God, surely because my flock became a prey, and my flock became meat to every beast of the field, because there was no shepherd, neither did my shepherds search for my flock, but the shepherds fed themselves, and fed not my flock; therefore, O ye shepherds, hear the word of the Lord; Thus saith the Lord God: Behold, I am against the shepherds; and I will require my flock at their hand, and cause them to cease from feeding the flock; neither shall the shepherds feed themselves any more; for I will deliver my flock from their mouth, that they may be meat for them..." (EZEKIEL, 34, 1-8).

The holier a place, the more terrible is the abomination of desolation in it. And since the holiest place upon earth is the Holy Orthodox Church built upon the Rock, Christ, and resting upon Christ's sons and brothers (MATT. 12, 50), Apostles and holy Fathers, it is easiest of all for the enemy (strange as this may seem at first glance) to devastate it.

Every sacred rite is a *great spiritual reality,* an embodiment of the Holy Spirit. As such it is never 'neutral,' but brings with it either Eternal Life or eternal death. External, formal, soulless use of sacred objects, words and actions generates and accumulates in the world deadly negative energy. A man who radiates such energy becomes a servant of antichrist. If a man is bedecked with gold and honoured with high rank, but his heart does not glow with the fire of penitence, love and prayer, one may truly say to him in the words of the Revelation: "Thou sayest, I am rich, and increased with goods . . . and knowest not thou art poor and blind and naked. I counsel thee to buy of me *gold tried in the fire*" (REV. 3, 17-18).

A purifying fiery calamity has befallen the Russian Church. The ways of Divine Providence are unfathomable. But calamities befall men for their salvation, and the Lord reveals their sins to them after sending the salutary calamity.

Of course the Orthodox people as a whole are responsible both for the decline of Orthodoxy in individuals and for the complete alienation from it of many souls. But most of the responsibility falls upon those who know more than the masses of the people—on bishops, priests and deacons.

They were appointed by the Lord Jesus Christ to be mediators between Him—the One Shepherd—and His flock, but proved for the most part to be a wall between Him and His people. "God shall smite thee, thou whited wall" were St. Paul's prophetic words to the High priest (ACTS 23, 3). And indeed, both that high priest and many others in the history of churches and nations were 'whited walls'—painted and outwardly seemly *walls* between God and God's people.

Seizing the key of understanding they neither went in themselves, neither suffered them that were entering to go in (MATT. 23, 13). They strained the gnat of ritual and formalism, and swallowed the camel of Christ's mercy and righteousness, humility and simplicity.

Not to live according to one's faith is worse than to live according to one's unbelief. No atheist can do the Church of Christ so much damage and bring so much devastation into its fold as an evil, money-loving priest who received, and has not been deprived of, the awe-inspiring grace of performing sacraments and wearing sacred vestments. It is they, those priests and bishops, who will say to the Lord at the Last Judgment: "Lord, Lord, have we not prophesied in Thy name and done many wonderful works?" (MATT. 7, 22-23) and the Lord, meek and gentle, will say to them: "Depart from me, *ye that work iniquity.*" Such 'workers of iniquity' include all the servitors of the Church who substitute grace-less pagan priesthood for Christ's gracious pastorship, who dominate the people instead of serving them. They look not after the weak but after the fat sheep and rejoice not at the sinners that repent (LUKE 13, 7-10) but at the righteous who have no need and no desire to repent, if those righteous bountifully support their bodily needs. Such pastors perform the holy rites of the Church like a heathen ritual, without faith, mercy, love or heart-felt prayer, without serving God in spirit and in truth.

Orthodox Church life with all its holy rites and rules is a great field for spiritual activity and an ever-increasing, vital force for those who have the will and vocation for true pastorship. But this wonderful churchliness becomes a stumbling block and a pitfall for those who do not approach it in the spirit of Christ's Priesthood and Christ's Kingdom.

Purifying the gold, the fire of the Divine Sacraments burns the straw.

It is easy for the weak human soul to be carried away by the *semblance of priesthood,* by the external performance of 'rites,'* musical singing, beauty of the surroundings and of words—by the whole setting of the Church,

---

* There are no figurative rites in the Church; there are only gracious realities of the Divine Kingdom.

by all its *corporeality* which, if not animated and inspired by the Spirit of Christ, becomes a sacrilege and represents Christ's dead, not risen, body. This is an abomination which has a *mystery* of its own (REV. 17, 5). And this is in truth the "abomination of desolation, spoken of by Daniel the prophet, standing where it ought not (let him that readeth understand)," of which the Saviour spoke and which to this day prevents many from receiving His Light.

Unworthy pastors lose the power of celebrating the Sacrament *themselves*: they are invisibly bound by an angel's hand which offers for consecration the believers' Holy Gift.

The most holy sacrament of the Eucharist is trampled upon and defiled not only by the 'sorcerers' (on whose account the Church discontinued the practice of giving the consecrated Elements into laymen's hands) but also by unworthy priests who both in their life and in their church services have neither the faith nor the will to be in the Lord or to have the Lord in them.

This is pagan priesthood devoid of grace and St. John Chrysostom was referring to it when he said, "I think many priests have no part in salvation." It is 'professionalism,' a profanation of the Holy. Life and the Holy Scripture show with a terrible reality that the clergy have at times lowered the standards of pastorship and indeed sunk beneath the level of ordinary human morality.

If they did not acknowledge the One Shepherd, how could they be shepherds of the flock? If they were not conscious of His interceding for them before God, how could they intercede for others? The people, sanctified according to the degree of their faith by the grace of the sacraments celebrated by them, went astray through coming into contact with these false shepherds and seeing their lives.

There are few souls in the world so enlightened by the spirit of Christ's wisdom that when they see an offending priest, they are not 'offended in Christ,' but cling to Christ and love the Church still more ardently, trying to serve more devotedly than ever the Lord Whom they see betrayed.

The majority of 'believers' at the least offence are shaken in their faith in the Church and even in God Himself. Such people easily fall away from the Church. They are the 'babes' in faith. We must not judge them severely, but help and *safeguard* them.

Truly "whoso shall offend one of these little ones which believe in Me, it were better for him that a millstone were hanged about his neck, and that he were drowned in the depths of the sea" (MATT. 18, 6).

Priesthood is a *great power of sanctification* ("a reservoir of grace" in the words of Fr. John of Kronstadt), but it may also be a great power for offence in this world.

Evil pastorship may be exercised by those who are given any degree of power over others: parents, guardians, leaders, rulers, chiefs, teachers, tutors, scientists, doctors, writers, journalists, actors. . . .Everyone of them, in his sphere unenlightened by the light of Christ, may act as a conductor for the devil's lies and persecute God's Truth in the world and in man.

The kingdom of the 'second death' (i.e. spiritual death —REV. 20, 14) makes proselytes just as the Kingdom of Life does—indeed much more insistently, for it is aggressive and insolent. Second death has a number of servants in the world, both conscious and unconscious. If earthly preachers alone were left on earth, it would have long ago become hell. But the first Evangelist upon earth was the Creator Himself in the Person of His Only Son. He,

the Lamb slain before the foundation of the world, crucified under Pontius Pilate and the priest-pastors Annas
and Caiaphas, Himself preaches His Truth in the world.
And no shouts or whispers of evil can stifle His voice or
diminish His love.

God's love, like sunlight, is shed upon all mankind,
and if some men flee from the life-giving sun to the damp
and gloomy cellars of their thoughts and feelings, can we
blame for it the Sun of Righteousness that shines "on the
evil and on the good"?

Some characteristics of evil pastorship.

I. *Love of Money; practical materialism; offering
prayers or sacraments on the payment of a fee*—which is
a sin and a perversion of God's Kingdom.*

II. *Pomp, show, theatricality*. . . (the angel warned
St. Hermas concerning false shepherds by saying: 'See
Hermas, wherever there is pomp, there is deceit' i.e.
falsity before God). The Orthodox rite is not pompous
or theatrical; it is a reverent and prayerful reality, calling unto God with voice, colour and movement—the surrender to God of all this world's flesh. Only through a
heart aglow with love for God and man does Orthodox
symbolism find its *right to truth* and become a heavenly
reality.

III. *Fawning on the rich and the powerful. A con-
temptuous attitude to poor and humble people. "Respect
of persons."* Timidity and false gentleness in denouncing

---

* Even if the priest is not personally interested in acquiring material
means through the Gifts of grace he must not allow this for his parishioners' sake, so as to instil in them a clear sense of God's *mercy* and of Divine
gifts which cannot be bought or sold and are incommensurable with earthly
values.

the sins of the mighty ones in this world. Rudeness and bad temper with subordinate and defenceless people.*

IV. *Preaching in church earthly values and attainments; absorption in some side-issue or work* to the detriment of the direct pastoral task of healing souls and bringing them to the One Shepherd. Lack of reverence in church.†

V. *Seeking honour and glory for oneself, vanity.* Signs of atheism: "How can ye believe, which receive honour one of another, and seek not the honour that cometh from God only?" Indication of pastoral faith: "he that seeketh his glory that sent him" (JOHN 5, 44).

VI. *Lack of care for the human soul.* . . . "He that is an hireling, and not the shepherd, whose own the sheep are not, seeth the wolf coming, and leaveth the sheep, and fleeth: and the wolf catcheth them, and scattereth the sheep" (JOHN 10, 12-13).

---

* It has a very painful effect on the laity when, because of some slight mistake, a higher cleric makes a rude reprimand to his subordinate during a church service. If a pastor does not spare the feelings of those at prayer, is he likely to care for their feelings outside the church?

† A certain layman came once to a refugee church at the very beginning of the Liturgy and saw through the open south door of the sanctuary that the priest while robing himself was comfortably talking to the reader on purely secular matters. The layman knew that the priest should put on his vestments *prayerfully,* and at once lost respect for this particular pastor not mindful of the holy things entrusted to him. If the priest during the service had preached an inspired sermon about the need for silence and reverence in church, could that layman have believed him? The Lord has said, however: "Whatsoever they bid you observe, that observe and do; but do not ye after their works" (MATT. 23, 3).

3

Good Pastorship

THIS MEANS—in the first instance "ministering spirits, sent forth to minister for them who shall be heirs of salvation" (HEB. 1, 14).

The Lord "maketh his angels spirits, His ministers a flaming fire" (Ps. 104).

The whole of the Revelation is full of instances of the communion between earth and heaven. As Jacob saw, angels are "ascending and descending. . . ." We are constantly shown glimpses of angels, God's servants, pastors, teachers, leaders, messengers, warriors.

Angelic help is revealed to men, waking or sleeping, in a variety of circumstances. "Twelve legions of angels" are ever ready to rush down to the earth in defence of the Name of Christ, the Only and Beloved (alas, not of all men), Son of God and Son of man.

Every human being is surrounded by incorporeal powers and to everyone invisible guardian angels are sent, speaking in the depths of a pure conscience of salvation (a defiled conscience is deaf to the voice of heaven), pointing out to man his way among life's difficult circumstances, both external and inward.

Guardian angels include not only spirits who never

lived on earth but also the departed spirits of the righteous, a small number of whom have been canonized by the Church. This has been done for the purpose of invocation, confession and affirmation of the bond between heaven and earth (and not for the sake of bestowing earthly glory on the dwellers in heaven who do not seek such glory and suffer from it rather than rejoice in it; their only glory and joy is that the Lord Jesus Christ in the Holy Trinity should be glorified in men; they work for this glorification and have wholly devoted themselves to it). The Song of Praise to the "Holy Angel, the watchful guardian of human life" reveals in every line of it the essence of angelic service. Every earthly pastor could learn from it *the spirit of his pastoral service*.

Earthly teachers and pastors who truly teach men the one thing needful,—the one thing necessary for eternity—are like their heavenly spiritual leaders and teachers in everything except in being in the flesh and liable to sin. This applies, first of all, to pastors who have received the apostolic grace through the laying on of hands—bishops, presbyters and deacons. The latter are ordained not solely for assisting in church services, but also for helping the priest in preaching the Gospel and testifying to the truth. Servers are not merely banner-bearers, readers and singers, but in a like measure witnesses to the faith and defenders of the Church both in their lives and in knowing how to defend the true faith and to attract the indifferent and the unbelieving to the Church. The grace of *cheirothesia* is given them for this, as well as for praying.

Every Christian, too, is a teacher in so far as, in St. Peter's words he must "always be ready to give an answer to every man that asketh you a reason of the hope that is in you with meekness and fear." Acts of the faith always *teach,* even if the agent remains silent.

But the responsibility of being teachers attaches in particular to parents in relation to their children, to rulers in relation to citizens, to judges in relation to those on trial and to chiefs in relation to their subordinates. In a broad sense, artists, writers, composers, university professors are teachers too. Their moral and spiritual responsibility before God increases in proportion to their fame, for the words or actions of a well-known man may edify many, or lead them astray.

In real Orthodox culture pastorship must be highest in the hierarchy of teachers who spread the light of Christ in the hierarchy of teaching which spreads the light of Christ in the world and transmits Divine wisdom.*

But in order to be truly the salt of the world, of every layer of it, priesthood must not be a class or caste: pastors must come from every section of society. This is an external condition and the Russian Church is reaching it through the fire of terrible trials. But the inner and far more important condition is that the priest must be *spiritually above* his flock. It happens (and not infrequently) that instead of leading his flock up to heaven, he brings them still closer to the earth.

A pastor must not be 'worldly.' Over-indulgence in food, drink and sleep, idle talkativeness, playing cards and other games, visiting places of amusement, absorption in political questions of the day, belonging to a party or to some worldly organization—all this is inadmissible for a priest. He must have an attitude of serene impartiality toward all men, and approach them in the spirit of the Gospel. Taking part in secular earthly unions seething with suman passions—even if these unions be of the noblest kind—makes a pastor 'carnal' and earthly instead

---

* *Direct* transmission is through prayer and open profession of faith. *Indirect* transmission is through the person's general inner attitude—scientific, artistic, or practical—revealing his faith or preparing the ground for faith.

of spiritual, causes him to misjudge people and be partial, blunts the keenness of his vision and indeed may blind him altogether.

Evangelical "unworldliness" ("in the world, but not of the world") must be characteristic of every pastor and his church-helpers. Only through being unworldly, unfettered by any earthly values, whether material or ideological, can a pastor become *free in Christ*. "If the Son shall make you free, ye shall be free indeed" (JOHN 8, 36). It is a pastor's vocation *to liberate* souls for the Kingdom of God, and he must in the first instance be himself free from the power of the world, the flesh and the devil.

Liberation from the world. Standing outside all earthly party organizations, above all secular disputes, not only formally but inwardly, a pastor must be impartial to all—the distinguished and the humble, the poor and the rich, the young and the old, the beautiful and the hideous. In all human intercourse he should have concern for a man's immortal soul. A pastor must be easy to approach by men of every shade of opinion. He must know that the invisible enemy will take advantage of his every worldly tie, even if it be not sinful, in order to wound him, to hinder his work, to prevent men, whose views are different from his, from seeking his prayers or going to confession to him. These men will of course have themselves to blame for not having been able to overlook the priest's personal opinions, but the priest will not feel any better for knowing that the fault lies *not only* with him; he is there not for the strong but for the weak, and must do all he can to help every soul to be cleansed and enter the Church. Much that is permissible for a layman is sinful for a priest.

A pastor's aim is to be a true 'spiritual father,' to lead all men to the One Heavenly Father, and of course he must do his utmost to make himself equally close to all, and all equally close to him.

Liberation from the flesh. If the spiritual conception of 'flesh' and 'carnality' means not the physical body, but the preponderance of carnal life over the spiritual, and man's enslavement by the forces of his body which "quench the spirit," it is of course as necessary to be liberated from 'the flesh' as from "the world."

A priest must not be an evident and strict ascetic. That would *frighten* many, and turn them against spiritual life. *The invisible enemy frightens people* with the idea of 'spiritual life' confusing it in their minds with "mortification of the body" and other ideas terrifying and unbearable to a simple layman. And people turn away from all spiritual life, alarmed at the spectre of 'asceticism.' Hence, a priest must not *appear,* and still less, of course, show himself to be a strict ascetic. Feeling this, some priests fall into the opposite sin and, under the guise of humility and of abasing themselves before others by 'not appearing to be different from them,' weaken and kill themselves by incontinence — and actually pride themselves (inwardly, and sometimes even outwardly) on such 'humility.' The humility is of course purely illusory and in truth is sheer prevarication. Putting aside, one must make *modest use of earthly goods necessary for life.*

A pastor's spiritual and prayerful life will itself indicate to him the right measure of abstinence. Every superfluity is *instantly* reflected upon the inner state of a man who is spiritual and strives always to be prayerful, light, ready to do good and free from the dark, hesitant and oppressive thoughts that invariably beset the soul as the result of incontinence in drink,* food and sleep.

---

* Wine is not forbidden by the Divine commandments, but if it is a temptation, better not drink it at all. In parishes where the clerics have given offence to the laity by such incontinence, it is essential that the priests should for the sake of the Church and for rehabilitating priestly dignity give up wine altogether, as a kind of penance for their brethren.

26

A singer fasts for six hours before a performance so as to feel 'light' and to make the most of his voice. A boxer strictly follows a certain regime and while keeping his body strong takes care not to make it too heavy. This is true, practical, medical asceticism—a condition of health and of the fullest vitality.

A pastor, and indeed every Christian, cannot fail to practice such asceticism, since unlike an earthly fighter, he is *constantly* struggling himself, with his sinfulness, and with the invisible incorporeal enemy who takes advantage of his smallest lapse or carelessness—especially of a priest's; St. Peter has well described this (I PETER 5, 8). Spiritual experience teaches us best how to struggle with the body for the sake of the holy and blessed freedom from passions.

Liberation from the devil: "This kind goeth not out but by prayer and fasting" (MATT. 17, 21).

For those who live in the world fasting is abstinence. The essence of fasting is not defined by the external rules laid down by the Church. The Church merely *admonishes* fasting and determines when it should be specially remembered (Wednesdays and Fridays, the four yearly fasts and so on). Everyone must define for himself the extent of fasting so that the body should receive its due, and the spirit should grow, abiding in peace and equanimity. This peace ("Peace I leave with you, my peace I give unto you; not as the world giveth, give I unto you"— John 14, 27) is a region to which the evil one cannot attain. The evil spirit, a spiritual thief and robber, tries first of all to disturb a man's equanimity, "to upset" and "revolt" him. When he succeeds in disturbing the crystal clear well of the soul and raising slime from the bottom through some temptation or obsession (most often through another person), he begins to fish in the troubled waters of the soul and incite the man, *weakened by pas-*

sion (of anger, lust, envy, greed) to transgress, i.e. to violate Christ's law. And if the man does not break this cobweb by prayer and penitence, it will soon become a string and then a rope and finally a chain binding him like a convict to the barrow carting evil about the world. He will become a tool of the evil one. The service and sonship of God is replaced first by the service, and then by the sonship of the devil.

It is a rule of spiritual warfare to subdue every passion by the power of Christ immediately, as soon as it has arisen. We cannot banish it completely at once, but we can drive it "to the bottom" so that it will die there under the influence of the waters of grace and our soul will always be serene, peaceful, loving, spiritually sober, awake, and full of goodwill. If 'a breach' threatens or actually happens in some region of the soul, we must direct our whole attention upon it and by 'force,' i.e. by prayerful struggle restore the peace of heart and soul ("The Kingdom of heaven suffereth violence and the violent take it by force," said the Saviour referring to the Kingdom of God which on earth is acquired or lost *within* man). This is spiritual sobriety. A spiritually sober man need not fear the enemy. "Behold I give unto you power to tread on serpents and scorpions, and over all the power of the enemy" (LUKE 10, 19). The enemy is terrible and dangerous only to the slothful, lazy and spiritually feeble. No righteousness will avail such men. If one does any number of heroic deeds in a war but ends by treachery, they will be worthless. "He that shall endure unto the end, the same shall be saved." If a man, and especially a priest, devotes as much care to guarding his soul as the enemy uses for ruining it, he can certainly feel secure. In the depths of his free and peaceful heart he will always, even amidst great trials, hear the reassuring voice: "It is I; be not afraid" (MATT. 14,27).

A pastor is a spiritual architect—a builder of souls, constructing out of these souls the House of God—the communion of peace and love, "for we are labourers together with God" (I Cor. 3, 9). It is the greatest, the most blessed work to take part in building the Kingdom of God. Spiritual enlightenment enables one—especially a priest—to be not a servant "who knoweth not what his lord doeth" but a son in the house of the Father, entering into his Father's work. A pastor's psychology is that of a husbandman and gardener. Every blade of corn is a human soul; every flower is a human being.

A good pastor knows his *farm,* understands the processes of organic life and knows how to further them. He looks at every plant and takes care of it. His work is to prepare and till the soil, to sow seed, to water the plants, to weed, to graft good stock onto wild stock, to spray the vines, to protect the fruit from thieves and birds, to watch over its ripening and harvest it in due season . . . .

A pastor's knowledge is that of a *physician* who can diagnose a disease, apply various methods of treatment, prescribe and even make up the necessary medicines. A correct diagnosis of the disease, a proper analysis of the organism and its various psychical secretions is a pastor's first task.

A pastor has a spiritual medicine chest by him: plasters, bathing lotions, cleansing and smollient oils, drying and healing powders, disinfectants, tonics, a surgical knife (to be used in extreme cases only).

A good pastor is a warrior and a commander; a helmsman and a captain, a father, mother, brother, son, friend, servant; a carpenter, a polisher of precious stones, a gold seeker; a writer writing the Book of Life.

True pastors, like pure mirrors of the Sun of Righteousness, reflect for mankind the radiance of heaven and give warmth to the world.

Those pastors may also be likened to sheepdogs guarding the flock of the One Shepherd. A good and intelligent sheepdog zealously runs around the flock and, always gentle with the sheep, pushes with its nose every sheep that lags behind, driving it to the rest of the flock; but as soon as danger appears it is transformed from a peaceful dog into a fierce one. Everyone who has seen this will understand the true behaviour of a pastor of Christ's flock.*

Good pastorship is the power of the One Good Shepherd, which has been poured out into the world and has found sons — sons "according to its heart." "And I will give you pastors according to mine heart, saith the Lord, which shall feed you with knowledge and understanding" (JER. 3, 15). Great was the light shed by *those pastors* in the world as recorded in their deeds and words —addressed to the world and to the pastors in it:

"The elders which are among you I exhort, who am also an elder, and a witness of the sufferings of Christ, and also a partaker of the glory that shall be revealed: feed the flock of God which is among you, taking the oversight thereof, not by constraint, but willingly, not for filthy lucre, but of a ready mind; neither as being lords over God's heritage, but being examples to the flock. And when the chief Shepherd shall appear, ye shall receive a crown of glory that fadeth not away" (I PETER 5, 1-4).

". . . be thou an example of the believers, in word, in conversation, in charity, in spirit, in faith, in purity. Till I come, give attendance to reading, to exhortation, to doctrine. Neglect not the gift that is in thee, which was given thee by prophecy, with the laying on of the hands of the presbytery. Meditate upon these things; give thy-

---

* With remarkable profundity the Bible calls timid, unreliable, lazy pastors *dogs that do not bark*. "His watchmen are blind; they are all ignorant, they are all dumb dogs, they cannot bark, sleeping, lying down, loving to slumber" (Is. 56, 10).

self wholly to them; that thy profiting may appear to all. Take heed unto thyself, and unto the doctrine; continue in them: for in doing this thou shalt save thyself, and them that hear thee" (I TIM. 4, 12-16).

"... I put thee in remembrance that thou stir up the gift of God, which is in thee by the putting on of my hands. For God hath not given us the spirit of fear; but of power, and of love, and of a sound mind' (II TIM. 1, 6-7).

What is there to add to this? everything has been said so simply and forcibly by the chief apostles. But to show forth the apostolic revelation about pastorship is the work of a lifetime and therefore — of many words directed to the good and of expressing the old and the eternal in a new way and applying it to the new conditions under which the Church lives and suffers.

PART ONE

1

Vocation

A PASTOR must be called to his work by God. To strive for apostolic hands to bring down Divine grace upon a man who has not been called, but seeks priesthood for earthly reasons and considerations, is the inqiuity of Simon Magus (even if it involves no simony). Divine grace cannot be compelled, cannot be disposed of according to human will, especially if that will be sinful.

Everyone who is to be ordained or who seeks ordination must be spiritually tested by the bishops who will have to give answer to God for laying on hands.

As a rule the test is purely external and academic and concerns the theoretical knowledge of the Scriptures, Church history, canons and rites. But a seminary diploma or a theological degree does not in itself testify to a pastoral vocation. The call to pastorship is a Divine mystery known only in the depths of the man's conscience ("For what man knoweth the things of a man, save the spirit of man which is in him?" (I COR. 2, 11) and revealed to the spiritual insight of his confessor or of the bishop responsible for the ordination.

Some of the signs of vocation are the following:

1) A deep sense of one's unworthiness;
2) A sincere understanding of pastorship as sacrificial service and dedication of one's whole life to God;
3) A real spiritual experience of faith;
4) Experience in caring for the soul of another.

These are general signs. The call to true pastorship comes as a rule not only from the depths of the man's conscience but also through the help of those near him, who, inspired from above, persuade him to enter the path of pastoral service.

The mystery of vocation is profound and many-sided, and it is impossible to define all of its aspects. The only essential thing to say is that it must always confront the man called to priesthood, and he must face it, putting aside all his human desires and waiting for the ways of Providence.

2

Ordination

THROUGH THE HANDS of the apostle-bishop the Divine energy of the Holy Spirit descends upon the head and the whole person of the ordained. "Thy hands have made me and fashioned me" (Ps. 119, 73). Just as man is the creation of God's hands (i.e. powers or energies), so priesthood is created and accomplished in the sacrament of ordination by the hand of God through the hands of the apostle-bishop.

During the singing of the Cherubic hymn the man to be ordained is, like a bridegroom, led three times round the altar while the marriage troparions are sung:

"Ye holy martyrs who have fought the the good fight and obtained the crown, pray unto the Lord for the salvation of ours souls.

"Glory be to Thee, O Christ our God, the praise of the Apostles and the joy of the martyrs, whose preaching was the consubstantial Trinity.

"Exult, O Isaiah, for a Virgin has conceived and brought forth a Son, Emmanuel, God and man, The East is His name; Him do we magnify, and call the Virgin blessed."*

---

* The prayers are quoted from John Glen King's translation, 1772.

34

The work of priesthood is to propagate the gracious Blood of Christ in the world. Priests whose office it is to celebrate the sacrament of the Body and Blood are servants of Christ, suffering 'even unto blood' (HEB. 12, 4) and bearers of His blood amidst the flesh and blood of this world. They are the blood which vivifies the Body of the Church.

It is noteworthy that the rite of ordination begins not with petitions, but with the solemn profession of the fulfillment of God's will. The Lord has chosen a servant, and will forthwith pour down His gifts upon him. The Church begins by giving glory to God, and the earthly Church merely beseeches the Heavenly for the salvation of him who ordains and of the ordained.

After going round the holy table three times, kissing its corners and making an obeisance to the bishop, the man to be ordained kneels and clinging to the holy table covers his face with his hands (as it were in shame and fear of his unworthiness* commending his whole life into the hands of God. And the bishop, the bearer of the Divine authority, laying his hands on the ordained's head, says:

"The Divine grace which healeth our infirmities and supplieth our defects promoteth (N), the most pious† deacon to the order of a presbyter: let us pray for him, that the grace of the Holy Spirit may come upon him."

"Lord, have mercy upon us," the Church calls out thrice. The senior priest present then says a special litany which includes petitions for: "Our bishop (N), for the priesthood, for protection, for abiding peace, health, salvation and for the work of his hands" and for "the servant of God (N) now ordained to the priesthood, and

---

* Before being ordained deacon (the first degree of the holy orders) the man confesses the sins of his whole life.

† These words must correspond to the reality.

for his salvation." Meanwhile the bishop recites a secret prayer, and then, still holding his hands on the head of the ordained, says aloud the final prayer:

"O God, great in power, unsearchable in wisdom, and wonderful in Thy counsels towards the sons of men, O Lord Who hast been pleased to grant unto this Thy servant the order of a presbyter, replenish him with the gifts of Thy Holy Spirit: that he may be worthy to stand before Thy holy altar unblameably, to preach the Gospel of Thy kingdom, to minister the word of Thy truth, to present unto Thee spiritual gifts and sacrifices, and to renew Thy people by the laver of regeneration: that at the second coming of the great God and our Saviour Jesus Christ, Thine only begotten Son, he may receive the reward of the faithful servant of his Lord's house, through the multitude of Thy goodness."

And — *Glory.*

This prayer indicates the pattern of pastoral action— of the blessed divinely-human work, carried on by man through the grace of Christ.

Five powers should be exercised by a priest:

I. To stand before the Altar of Redemption offering his own *life as a sacrifice;*

II. To spread in the world the Gospel of Christ's Kingdom. To proclaim the Lord Jesus Christ as the only true Judge and King of the world;

III. To manifest the Truth as holy: to show it as applying to all occasions and circumstances, to bear witness to Christian righteousness on every path of life;

IV. To bring spiritual gifts and sacrifices: to work "in the sweat of the brow" of one's soul. To celebrate the Liturgy — the bloodless Sacrifice of praise and thanksgiving for everything;

V. To manifest to the world the Divine Fatherhood (as a symbol of this the priest assumes the appellation of a 'spiritual father'). To baptize with water, the Holy Spirit and the fire of faith in the name of the Holy Trinity. To give men birth into a new life —to bring about their spiritual birth.

The sacrament of ordination is concluded with the repeated exclamations by all the clergy and the people "Axios!" ("Worthy!"), which indicate that the whole Church community, symbolizing the Bride, takes part in the Sacrament.

After the consecration of the Holy Gifts, the bishop puts into the hands of the newly ordained pastor a particle of the Body of Christ, with the words: "Take this token and preserve it. Thou shalt be called to give answer for it at the second and glorious coming of our Lord Jesus Christ." And bending over Christ's most pure Body which lies in his hand, the priest prays to the Lord of Hosts to give him love and bless his priestly service.

3

Education

THE MORE SPIRITUAL the pastor is, the less important
becomes his education, his formal knowledge. The
pastor must be "educated" from above, by the Spirit
given him at ordination. The power of the Cross is a
result of an inner self-crucifixion. The true spirituality
is *universality*. And the saints are truly universal men,
for they know the essential and, therefore, everything
else. The question from which school St. John of the
Ladder or St. Seraphim of Sarov graduated, or what
thesis Fr. John of Kronstadt wrote is obviously a secondary one. In the history of the Church there are men of
great learning—St. Cyprian of Carthage, St. Athanasius
the Great and also simple and uneducated men — St.
Nicholas and St. Spyridon. The learned Apostle Paul
stands together with the simple Apostle Peter, the well-
educated Prophet Daniel—with a shepherd, the Prophet
Amos. All this reveals the simple truth that worldly
learning must neither be depreciated nor considered the
criterion of wisdom and spirituality.

Theological education is extremely valuable and has
a great importance but only if through the entire struc-

ture of the theological school genuine faith shines through. Seminaries must not only educate but also *form* the pastor. After each lecture the seminarian must know *more* and also love the truth more, believe more in its Source and Fulness, Our Lord Jesus Christ, the Alpha and the Omega of life and knowledge.

In the existing pluralism and complexity of philosophical, religious and pseudo-religious teachings, the Orthodox pastor must be like a "many-eyed Cherubim," seeing all aspects and the spiritual weight of each doctrine. The true theological education supplies us with genuine criteria of Truth, with the possibility to discern the good and the evil; it widens the intellectual and emotional horizons of man, as if some spiritual x-rays were piercing through both wisdom and pseudo-wisdom of this world, giving each of them their real place.

The inevitably *abstract* character of all knowledge, even spiritual knowledge, must be overcome by the personal spiritual life of the pastor. Many have truly closed the door of the Kingdom to themselves and to others by abstract truth. For the one having faith and knowing the ways to increase it, abstract knowledge as well as the knowledge of anti-Christian doctrines are not dangerous. The Saviour spoke of this problem in MARK 17-18. The first aim of theological schools is to supply weapons against anti-Christian and pseudo-Christian ideas, which have two horns, like the Lamb (text from REVELATION 13, 2). Of special value for the pastor is the "liberal arts" secular education, which prepares for the organic appropriation of the Truth in a theological school. The Pastor must know the Truth not only intellectually, in the abstract manner, but with his "whole heart," "whole soul," "whole strength" and "whole understanding" (LUKE 10, 27). Only such a Truth may be the generation of man's life and his first joy.

Truth is joyful. And its knowledge cannot but be joyful. This is an important aspect of Christian education. The pastor who has learned in the seminary chapel and classroom this joyful approach to Truth will certainly bring reverent joy into his pastoral ministry and into the hearts of men. Only the possessor of such living faith, the practitioner of the "internal peace" will—upon completion of his academic preparation—be full of it forever. And even if he becomes a bishop, the bearer of the Church's truth, or a learned theologian, he will never consider himself a "specialist," but "forgetting what is behind," he will "tend towards the goal, the honor of the high calling," in a never-ceasing desire to reach it, as it was reached by Christ Jesus (PHILIP. 3, 13-14).

A self-satisfied knowledge is pseudo-knowledge. And even Orthodox teaching in a self-satisfied mind will be pseudo-gnosis.

The graduates of a theological school know that they have laid only a first foundation. It is indeed a great achievement to know one's limitations and one's spiritual poverty. Knowledge *about God* is but a way to the knowledge *of God*.

4

Pastoral Spirituality

A PASTOR IS CALLED to do his work in different cultural layers of society. His pastorship will be much easier for him if he can adapt himself to the intellectual level of each one of them—being a philosopher with philosophers, and simple with the simple. In China, the Chinese language is used for preaching, and in Russia—Russian. Similarly, in visiting different families and entering different domains of culture, the pastor must know how to speak to every man in a language he understands. In our age the gift of "diverse kinds of tongues" (I Cor. 12, 10) means the gift of coming close to every human soul and making use of its ideas, its psychology. "He that is spiritual judgeth all things, yet he himself is judged of no man" (I Cor. 2, 15), i.e. a spiritual man has insight into human souls in spite of the differences in their culture, upbringing, education, moral character and disposition. If one may say so, a true pastor always speaks to a man in that man's language and not in his own. He is "made all things to all men" so that he may "by all means save some" (I Cor. 9, 22); "unto the Jews" the pastor becomes "as a Jew . . . to them that are under the law, as under the law" (I Cor. 9, 20). This shows love and understanding of God's work, and the priest is in this respect like an angel who always speaks to the conscience of every man, carefully considering human individuality, its special characteristics, its powers and its weaknesses. At confession and in giving spiritual advice it is particularly important to approach each person as a particiular individual and not in the abstract, not according to one's own theories. It is in this that the depth of pastoral love and wisdom shows itself.

There must be nothing conventional, 'customary,' theoretical about a priest's spiritual advice. It must be fresh and warm every time, springing from actual contact with this or that individual human soul. A pastor is a fine artist, a sculptor dealing not with marble, but with the precious and intangible material of heart and mind. He has to bring out the Divine *likeness* in the darkened Divine image. God has given him the power to do so, and if the man whom he is tending gives it to him also (by accepting his spiritual guidance), he cannot fail to carry out his task. The pastor's work is then done under favorable conditions: the sheep hears the shepherd's voice, and if the shepherd rightly passes on to that sheep the voice of the chief Heavenly Shepherd, the Kingdom of God is realized in man.

The pastor has still another task: to attract the soul that has strayed, surrendered itself to the spirit and ideas of this world, lured by the champions and exponents of that spirit. The pastor then has to follow the way of the Cross, struggling for that soul, suffering for it, praying for it . . . and using every opportunity to draw it away from the wrong path and direct it to the right one. "Except the Lord build the house, they labor in vain that build it." The soul is saved when the will of God meets the will of man and captivates it. The will of the pastor, captivated by the Divine will, must in its turn carry the will of another man to a meeting with the will of God. How multifarious are the stages and aspects of the struggle to save a soul!

The pastor comes to see that he has to wrestle not only with the evil human will (which is seldom *wholly* evil), but, in truth, with the evil will of demons as well. The full force of the 6th chapter of St. Paul's Epistle to the Ephesians is revealed to him, and he begins to understand more clearly and more fully than ever before that his whole personal experience, skill and knowledge, even all his faith, are of little avail in the struggle against these dark forces, apart from the grace which comes from above; that only the grace of the Holy Spirit is the true force and fulfillment of all his hopes and wishes as a priest. Far from making him passive, this conviction gives him especial daring. Having no hope in his own power and experience, he comes to trust in the power of God and to know that "when I am weak, then I am strong" (II Cor. 12, 10). He makes every effort, since "The Kingdom of Heaven suffereth violence and the violent take it by force"—take it not only for themselves but for another as well. Our 'violence' is prayerful love of God and man, realized in life — love, in answer to which the Divine blessing descends upon the world.

A priest believes that every heart-felt prayer reaches God (though it may not be fulfilled in accordance with our wishes). And, similarly, every pastoral effort helps to build up the Kingdom of God. The priest's hidden work includes *penitence* for the sinners. To develop the faculty of feeling penitence on another's behalf, the priest must, each time that he hears about sin or sees it, turn his mental gaze to the throne of God and say, "Lord, forgive him . . . Lord, cleanse and strengthen Thy servant." Through the practice of *intercession*, it becomes a holy habit of the heart not to condemn a sinner, but to commiserate with him, heaving at least a sigh of penitence on his behalf.

This pastoral love, hidden from the onlookers' eyes, rests upon the pastor's own practice of genuine penitence.

5

Purity

A PASTOR IS *soiled* not only if he stains his cassock and makes it dirty. He soils himself more by a thoughtless word, inordinate laughter, a vulgar joke or, worse still, by indulging in drink* or being addicted to smoking, by joining some purely secular organization and becoming a 'party man,' by behaving irreverently in church or out of it.† 'Pastoral purity' does not as such indicate purity of the heart — it merely means a pastor's correct behavior in the world, corresponding to the purpose of his calling. Its intrinsic mark is that the priest is conscious of the whole world as a temple of God, in which he is called to serve Him and, in diverse places and an infinite number of ways, to help human souls find the Kingdom of God and enter it.

---

* The present author knows of a certain parish among the Russian exiles where the parishioners, on entering the church, could unmistakedly tell by the priest's voice (even when he was saying liturgical prayers) whether or not he was sober. The parish of course was for several years deprived of a real pastorship and greatly deteriorated in consequence. And yet people went to confession and communion—a vivid instance of human long-suffering and of the *invisible pastorship* of the One Shepherd. (Thanks to the wisdom of the bishop, the situation in this parish was improved.)

† The purity of pastoral office is also damaged by frequent sermons on material subjects, especially in church. Sometimes utterly impermissible

things are done: the priest himself goes round with the collection plate, even when wearing the felon (this happens in America). There is no need to say how much harm to the cause of religion is done by the priest's asking to be paid for this or that prayer. In places where this still happens, sectarianism flourishes and the godless have all the weapons they need for attacking the Church.

Parishes, too, should keep watch over their 'purity' and not organize dances, concerts of light music and gambling lotteries 'in aid of the church.' Aid to the church should be pure and based upon mercy and sacrifice and not upon the purchase of earthly pleasures; it cannot be considered from a purely material point of view. The possibility of sanctifying souls is not bought at the price of darkening them.

6

Preparation for Church Services

A PRIEST IS PREPARED for officiating in the church by his previous service in it and outside it. A priest's whole life prepares him for standing before the throne of God. "Prepare thyself for standing before the altar by continual inward prayer" (ST. JOHN CLIMACUS). Is it necessary to read the whole of the 'Office before the Communion'? Fr. John of Kronstadt, speaking about himself, says that he had made it a rule to read only the actual prayers before the Communion, included in the morning Office. But we know that Fr. John of Kronstadt practiced continual inward prayer, and that indeed his pastoral life was in itself a prayer. The whole of one's life can indeed be prayer even for a layman, and still more so for a priest. Sacraments, petitionary and penitential prayers, thanksgivings, prayers for the departed, contacts with seekers of God, talks about faith, sermons, words of comfort and encouragement, reading, contemplative withdrawal into oneself in gratitude or penitence — all this is the river of pastoral prayer, the changing scenery of its banks.

It is helpful to a layman, and all the more to a priest, to keep a Penitential Diary for the sake of frequently confessing before God voluntary and involuntary sins and being cleansed from them as soon as possible, for pacifying one's conscience and growing more sensitive to sin. All this is a preparation for service, and true service is the best preparation for the service of worship that is to follow. A prayerfully celebrated Liturgy prepares the pastor better than anything else for the next Liturgy. Accordingly, a set form of prayer must not be considered in the Old Testament Judaic spirit of legalism. A Christian pastor's prayerful 'duty' to God is not a duty under the old dispensation when men burdened themselves with various rules and ordinances and, unable to fulfill them, lived with a permanently guilty conscience. Failure to understand the living spirit of Divine commandments was inexcusable even in the Jews, and is still more so in a Christian priest.

A pastor's whole spiritual attitude must make it impossible for him 'to strain at gnats' and, like a hireling, to count the number of prayers. A son turns to his father without calculating how many words he 'must' say to him. A son *speaks* to his father, strives to be always with him and opens his heart to him, knowing that it is not by the number of spoken words and not even by their beauty that the father will gauge his love. To have a filial attitude toward prayer, to stand before God freely and not by compulsion is the constant striving of a true priest. He has no difficulty in beginning his devotions and finds it hard to break them off.

If a priest has not yet achieved this (through the constant practice of inward prayer) he must *force* himself every morning and every evening — not to repeat the set number of prayers, but prayerfully to stand before God and beseech Him for the gift of prayer itself.

A pastor's aim is not to carry out the prescribed rules of prayer, but *to pray.**

The 'Office' set forth in the prayerbook is a most valuable *material for prayer* — a spiritual nectar permeated with the Holy Spirit and passed down through the Fathers of the Church who had immediate knowledge of the Spirit. This material does not bind one and may be either shortened or, of course, increased. 'Legalistic' conscience is at peace only if all that is 'prescribed' has been performed. But a Christian conscience (and especially a priest's) is at peace only if it has had *God's answer,* be it to the shortest of prayers. Such calm conscience, at peace with God and freed by Him from all earthly duties is the best supplicant before God.

---

* There are cases when a priest avoids frequent celebrations of the Liturgy, believing that he cannot celebrate without first having read through all the prayers contained in the preparatory Office; and for various reasons ("no time" etc.) he thinks he cannot do this often. And he dries up spiritually, depriving himself of the waters of the Liturgy and denying them to others. He justifies his sloth by strict observance of 'the law.' It also often happens that a priest hastily reads through a part of the Office and leaves the rest unread through laziness, thus defiling his conscience; while celebrating the Liturgy he feels guilty—not because he has not prayed sufficiently, has not found peace, has not repented, has not entered the innermost depths of his heart, but because "he has not read to the end" such and such prayers. . . .This also is symbolic of a Judaic, formalistic attitude to prayer.

Thirdly, there are cases when a priest simply neglects devotional preparation set forth in the Office. Thoroughly worldly in spirit, having no desire to take even a few breaths of the prayerful air of heaven, the priest rattles through Liturgy like 'sounding brass or a tinkling symbal.' This is a real crime—against his own soul and the souls of the faithful who come for his prayers.

7

Ministry in the Church

T HE PURPOSE OF MINISTRY is to widen the Church beyond its material boundaries, to take it into the people's homes, into their souls. Not infrequently, the opposite happens: this world invades the Church. Perhaps in
our time it does so in less crude and striking a form than
in Jerusalem when the Lord made a scourge of small
cords and drove out of the temple oxen and sheep and
those who sold them; but in our age too the world enters
the holy precincts. Special services and even requiems
are sometimes still infected with earthly considerations,*
with dry officialdom, with 'tinkling cymbals,' immoder-
ate public prayers for so and so's worldly prosperity, flattery for someone's ears. If only we always defended and
extolled above all the memory and the Holy Name of the
Almighty crucified King, meekly born in Bethlehem,
opening Heaven to men that they might hear the angels'
choir of praise! All who come to church for the sake of
the Crucified Lord want to hear that praise rather than
any other.

A priest can always gauge the degree of his own prayerfulness by the way he celebrates the service in an empty

or almost empty church. If he feels the holy tremor of awe only when the church is full (or when some 'important' people are present), it means that his devotions are not deep enough and that he is tainted with worldliness.

Just as bees, gathering honey from the flowers of the field, take it to their hives, so human souls, after true prayer, take heavenly sweetness from the church to their homes and distribute it in the world.

Holy is the beauty of the Orthodox rite, of the ikons, the architecture, the singing. . . . But it is not so much by this beauty as by the prayerfulness of the celebrants and by the pious reverence of the worshippers that a man is attracted to the Church and made faithful to it.

---

* Here is a sad instance from the recent past: on Christmas day solemn services of thanksgiving were held in all the churches in Russia—of thanksgiving not for deliverance from the devil, sin and death, but from the French army in 1812. That was a clear manifestation of the spirit of this world, substituting a temporal and transitory triumph for one of universal significance—a betrayal of the Triumph of the Incarnation.

8

Servers and Singers

DURING THE SERVICE a pastor must be strict, rather than kind, toward the singers, the readers and the boys who serve in the sanctuary. Some singers and readers behave so irreverently that they actually prevent people from praying. The congregation will refrain from talking in church if they hear no conversations going on among the choir members, the servers and those in the sanctuary.*

The power of the worshippers' prayer is weakened by 'showy' professional singing.† Church singing (and reading) must not *distract* people, but help them to concentrate. The more reverent and prayerful the singers are inwardly, the more gracious is the power of their singing. A worshipper may be carried away by good, though theatrical, singing and even feel a certain sweet tremor, but he would be in error if he took this for prayer. Emotional tension as such is not prayer. Only after dismissing the agitation can we pass to prayer, just as after dismissing pictorial images can we rise to imageless, 'non-sensuous' prayer which transcends emotion. This process of ascending from the mental to the spiritual is greatly

51

furthered by the reverent and spiritual character of the singing. The singers' thoughts and feelings must correspond as much as possible to the content of the hymns and canticles. Sincerity, i.e. correspondence between the words and sounds and the frame of mind is the true fulfilment of the Orthodox culture, a real spiritual force apart from which the Church ceases to be the Church and becomes merely a semblance of it. "God is the King of all the earth: sing ye praises with understanding" (Ps. 47, 8). The need for singing and reading 'with understanding' concerns, of course, most of all the priest himself, but it has a direct bearing upon all who sing and read in church. Whether the choir is voluntary, or its members have to support their material existence by singing (which is also legitimate) — they must remember that they represent the choirs of angels.

---

* In some churches the choristers and readers are so demoralized that, for instance, they leave the church during the Six Psalms—to have a smoke! Even deacons sometimes do this. "O Lord, though our iniquities testify against us, do Thou it for thy name's sake" (JER. 14, 7).

Some clerics (and even priests) follow a mistaken practice of combing their hair in the sanctuary; the proper place for this is the vestry. As a rule, a cleric should do nothing in an enclosed sanctuary which he would not do in an open one.

† It is impermissible to advertise church services in the newspapers in the same way as concerts, i.e. mentioning which singers will sing the different items. Such things, done to this day, are 'old leaven,' an offence, a profanation of the holy.

9

Ministry in the Home

"MY SWEETEST SAVIOUR!" writes Fr. John of Kronstadt in his book *My life in Christ,* "having come down from heaven to serve mankind, Thou didst preach the word of the heavenly truth not only in the temple, but through cities and villages, shunning no one, entering people's homes, especially the homes of those whose heartfelt repentance Thou didst foresee with Thy Divine gaze. Thou didst not remain sitting at home, but went in loving communion with all. Grant us to be in such communion with Thy people, that we, pastors of Thy sheep, be not secluded in our homes as in a castle or a prison, going out only for services in church or in private homes, only as a duty, only with prayers learned by heart. May our lips be open for free discourse with our parishioners in the spirit of faith and love! May our Christian love for our spiritual children be revealed and strengthened through free, lively, fatherly conversation with them! Oh what sweetness, what bliss hast Thou, our Lord and infinite Love, concealed in the spiritual converse, warmed by love, between a spiritual father and his children in spirit! How can I fail to do my utmost

53

in striving for that bliss? And it is but a feeble beginning, a faint likeness of the heavenly bliss of love! We must particularly love the communion of charity, both material and spiritual. 'To do good and to communicate forget not' (HEB. 13, 16)."

This ministry in the home—visiting one's parishioners, coming to know their lives, their minds, establishing a spiritual contact with them — is a direct continuation of ministry in the church.

By visiting a family, "the church which is in the house," and praying in the home, the priest imparts new life to it, and renews the very sacrament of marriage which is constantly obscured by quarrels, slights, misapprehensions, mutual lack of understanding. The pastor *revives* the blessing given by the Church to the family. The family is revived and strengthened by the priest's prayer and conversation, by his blessing of the house and sprinkling it and them with holy water. . . .It is good if during his short visit he succeeds in bringing the talk round to the *chief thing,* and directly or indirectly* 'seasons' the people's minds with the spirit of Christ and gives some heavenly nourishment to them. If a pastor's visit brings no such nourishment it is, at best, aimless. When choosing the families to visit, he must select in the first instance, those "whose throats are parched" with spiritual thirst. This thirst, foretold by the prophet (AMOS 8, 11) has already begun in the world. When a true pastor comes, parishioners eager for "the chief thing," positively forget about food and drink and, as it were, 'sit at his feet' consulting him about their inner experiences. Others, wishing to show their affection rush

---

* By 'indirect' teaching I mean *unnoticeably* throwing Christian light upon this or that practical question. Even apart from reason and memory, the human soul has the faculty of noticing and adopting another person's attitude to life, especially a trusted person's.

at once to prepare tea and other refreshment, or, knowing beforehand that the priest is coming, have everything ready, and their chief concern is to offer him a good meal. This kind of love also gives joy to the pastor, but in a different way; it complicates and slows down his work. If the meal is a modest one, it is of course blessed; but the parishioners' desire—especially that of rich parishioners on festive occasions—to reduce all contact with their pastor to serving him abundant food, is a worldly and misguided kind of love.

True love for the pastor expresses itself in the desire to obtain spiritual strength and holiness through him and to pray with him. A priest who is a living witness to the Divine truth unconsciously accustoms his parishioners to think of God and of their souls every time they meet him. The very sight of him will cheer and comfort them. In his person people will find their memory of God and of their highest spiritual values. Such a love is bound to be a blessing both for the flock and for the shepherd.

But not in every home and not all the time can a pastor talk with people about spiritual things. He has to take part in ordinary everyday conversations too. It is legitimate and natural for him to do so, but he must exercise vigilance and, above all, take care that the spirit of the conversation is in no way darkened. With children one may talk about trifles, if it be in peace and love, and yet call forth good and bright feelings in them. Such are a pastor's everyday 'educational' methods with his spiritual children and the world around him.

10

Ministry in Society

WE LIVE AT A TIME when, on the one hand, the faithful as an organized body have withdrawn (and are precluded) from guiding the life of the community and the state, and on the other, when certain states show a clear desire to utilize the social activities of the faithful and the spiritual influence of the Church for their own earthly ends.

Under those conditions pastors must be both wise and 'harmless as doves' according to the Gospel injunction. A pastor's harmlessness means humility and absence of worldly and destructive criticism; and his wisdom must consist in courageously upholding the eternal verities of the Church in a modern society which is worse than pagan, because it is a society of renegades. A modern pagan is not the ideal pagan of antiquity who was seeking the Kingdom of God and had a new truth preached to him by the Apostles. A modern pagan in Christian countries is one who has renounced Christ, who hates the Gospel and will have nothing to do with it. But even such an apocalyptically 'cold' man (REV. 3, 15) is better than one who is 'lukewarm' and indifferent to all truth.

While allowing and blessing entirely contemplative life for souls which have a true vocation for it, a pastor opens to the rest of the faithful beneficent possibilities of influencing social and political life.

Free from all worldly 'modernity,' a pastor should know the conditions of modern life. Without joining any particular party, he must be prepared to have among his flock men of widely differing convictions and of mutually hostile parties.

Standing side by side before the holy Chalice such men must bring into their lives the spirit of unity with regard to the main thing. While disagreeing about social questions, they must never indulge in social hostility or seek to destroy — whether physically or morally — a person's soul.

A pastor is not a-political or neutral — he is meta-political, and seeks the City that is to come. That is why he must be free from worldly turmoil. His eyes must not be blinded with earthly dust, but, like an eagle's, must clearly discern from heavenly height the smallest detail of earthly reality.

A pastor is not 'outside life;' he is merely outside its vanities. His direct task is not to invent new methods of social organization, but to make the most of every given social organization in order to teach men to be faithful to God. He educates men in all conditions of life and on every path of it to be followers of Christ's spirit.

Like the Lord Jesus Christ Himself, a priest teaches men not what social forms they should adopt, but in what way they should relate to one another in society.

11

Family

As the Lord Jesus Christ is the Head of His Church, so the pastor is the head of his parish. As the Church is the Body of Christ, so the parish is the living spiritual 'body' of the pastor. When he partakes of the Holy Communion, the whole parish, in a measure, partakes of it too. Pastorship in the spirit of Christ is for the parish the pastorship of Christ Himself. Great is the mystery of pastoral intercession and it rests upon perfect love (See Exodus 32, 32). In virtue of this organic, consanguinous relation (through the Blood of Christ) between the priest and the parish, the parishioners can do much towards the fulfillment of the pastorship of the priest by their prayers, confession, communion, humility, sensitiveness, and by covering their father's nakedness should it be uncovered as in the case of the righteous Noah.

In addition to his spiritual family, a priest has a family after the flesh. By bestowing its blessing upon the sacrament both of the spiritual and the corporeal marriage and thus uniting the two, the Church shows that all the aspects of life blessed by it have the same purpose. In recent years men seeking ordination in the Russian

Church have often elected to remain unmarried; for "both they that have wives be as though they had none" (I Cor. 7, 29). In our apocalyptic times this is of value to the Church if the choice of celibacy is dictated by mature and sober reflection, i.e. if it has a truly spiritual basis. For other priests, however, and for their whole pastoral work the collaboration of a wife, fully aware of her responsible position, has been and will continue to be salutary.* Thus, a priest's wife may collaborate with him by taking charge of the Church School, or by doing charitable work in the parish; but her chief and essential help to her husband consists in organizing his material life, in safeguarding him from petty trivialities, in creating a pious and reverent atmosphere in the home and in being sensitive to the parishioners' needs. The activity of a priest's wife who does all this can be compared only to that of a guardian angel.

---

* It is sad to find instances to the contrary, when wife and children actually hinder a priest instead of helping him, and bring worldly vanity into the pastoral home. Thus, among the emigrés a priest's wife, provided with all the necessaries of life, began selling cosmetics within the parish boundaries to increase her private income. In other cases, however, pastors' wives have shown truly wonderful self-abnegation.

12

School

THE SCHOOL, like the family, is an organic part of the pastor's world. The pastor's task is to bring into the school the influence of the Spirit of light. In the school where he teaches both masters and pupils are his children. Just as there may be disobedient children in a class, so among the teachers in a secular school there may be unbelievers, people who are outside the Church. A pastor cannot fail to extend his care and prayers to them also.

Teaching religion in secular schools almost always involves difficulties for a priest. True, there still exist some schools which may be said to be 'on the side of the Church,' but they are few in number. As a rule, in teaching their various subjects, schoolmasters — crudely or subtly — sow in the children's minds the seeds of discord between faith and knowledge. Hardly any think it necessary to explain to their pupils the difference between the domain of faith or spiritual knowledge and that of material knowledge — as University professors in Western Europe do if they happen to be believers.

In present day Russia teachers perform the demonic task of deliberately destroying the children's religious faith by sophisms intended to demonstrate the alleged contradictions between religion and 'exact knowledge.'

A priest teaching Scripture in a school must on no account confine himself to the formal and, for the most part, colorless school syllabus; he must be in close and living contact with his pupils, and above all, *interest* them as one who understands their minds and does not deaden them by his 'schoolmasterly' attitude. In school, as elsewhere, a priest should be a teacher of life, ready with a response to the questionings of a child's mind.

A priest teaching Scripture in a school must not only reveal to his pupils the true nature of religion, but must also 'inoculate' them, so to speak, against the poison of materialism which pervades modern life and science.

His hour at the school should not be a formal 'lesson' but rather a talk, an exchange of ideas. He must bear in mind that if Scripture lessons bore the children and make them dislike the subject, they may fight shy of religion for the rest of their lives.

Is it permissible to give marks for such religious conversation-lessons? Yes, it is, provided it not be done on the basis of the pupils' theoretical knowledge, but rather on psychological grounds—for the pupils' spiritual benefit. The teacher's liberality must make the children feel that it is *easy* to get high marks for Scripture: but a pupil's negligence must certainly be brought to light by a candidly unsatisfactory mark — which may, again, easily be replaced by a high one through diligence and good behavior.

The pupils should have a feeling that every lesson of Scripture is something *exceptional*; it should be unlike all other lessons, in which merely external discipline and external knowledge are required.

The spirit and methods of pastoral teaching at schools greatly need reform.

Purely religious schools (on Saturdays or Sundays) are extremely valuable for the parish. To create and develop them is truly Orthodox work — they are the Church's answer to the secularization of life and of education.

13

Confession

IN THE WORDS of Fr. John of Kronstadt confession is the 'touchstone' of pastoral love. A priest must have much love, patience, attention and care for the soul which comes to be healed (as the prayer before confession puts it), if he is to cure the penitent's wound. Some confessions are made with such profound contrition that nothing is left to the priest but thankfully to pronounce the absolution, meditating upon the power of penitence and God's mercy to the human soul. After such confessions a true pastor always feels a heavenly joy in his heart (LUKE 15, 7). But there are other confessions which are a pain to him: the penitents have nothing to say: they are either silent or use commonplace phrases such as: "There is nothing special," "I am a sinner like other people," etc. A lazy pastor is glad of such confessions, and is annoyed when a penitent displays too much zeal and is too sensitive to spiritual experiences (incomprehensible to a less developed mind).

It is a great mistake for a priest to imagine that everyone who comes to him for confession is *therefore* on a spiritually lower level than himself and needs directing.

As has already been said, many of the laity are spiritually deeper and more sensitive than the pastor to whom they come, wishing to receive the grace of the sacraments. A priest may fail to understand this, and unconsciously substitute himself, his own mind, for grace, sometimes actually damaging the precious seedlings of spirituality by his crude questions and advice.

A priest should know that his duty is to help and not to judge or to 'be a lord over God's heritage' (I PETER 5, 3); and above all he must win a man's spiritual confidence. It would be a mistake to base pastoral authority solely upon the external grounds of rank and office (that is the Roman Catholic standpoint). The authority of an Orthodox priest rests not only upon his rank but also on the practice of his fatherly love for a man's soul, on real spiritual power. It is this power, and not domain over man, that is given to priests; and spiritual power is a talent which, unless it be increased through the practice of fatherly love, loses its potency. Priests are given the power not to dominate over, or to bind human freedom, but to help its true development, to *educate* it. Such is the path for Orthodox priests and bishops. Some of them fall into the error of 'lording it over' God's heritage. They are like inexperienced gardeners who pull at the stems of plants and flowers to help their growth, but in fact simply pull them out. A priest must know that growth is the work of the Divine grace, through sunshine, warmth, light, air, food, water, dew—and the task of the gardener-priest is merely to weed the plants in God's garden and to water them with the waters of the sacraments.

Hence, the central moment in confession is the absolution given to the penitent, and effective only in so far as he truly repents.

A careful, attentive and reverent priest can do great and wonderful things to a man who is not aware of his own sins and yet comes to confession. He can help a soul to find its penitential depth. By the oil of love the priest, like an experienced physician, can re-establish in a sick soul, hardened in sin, the right feeling about life, the right attitude to its sins and to its immortal human dignity. When there are many penitents, it is a good thing to say, before confession, a few heartfelt words, and point out the necessity of forgiving others; then to indicate the various aspects of sinfulness and advise the people to confess first of all that which burdens their conscience most and be sure to put it into words.

Few laymen understand to the full the spiritual significance of verbally confessing their sins. A sin which a penitent felt 'shy' of confessing will certainly remain like a thorn in his soul and in time set up an inflammation, perhaps with fatal results. Only a confessor who has a truly compassionate, sympathetic love for men and fervent, fatherly zeal for their souls may, when necessary, rebuke a sinner. Only he who really knows man's spiritual structure and whose hand is firm when holding the fearful blade of God's rebuking words can be a skillful spiritual surgeon. In the words of St. Basil the Great, spiritual love is imperfect if at the right moment it does not venture to grieve the loved one for his own benefit. But an unskillful denouncer (one not moved by love) is a 'striker' (I TIM. 3, 3; see Apostolic Canons 27) and his lancet is not a surgical instrument, but a weapon.

The chief of the specifically pastoral sins are love of power, ambition and envy. A pastor has to wage unceasing battle against these enemies of his soul. How is he to do it? By constant sober vigilance over his feelings; by going to confession as often as possible.* A priest who neglects his own confession will never have the gracious

---

* Even if it has to be done in writing, because of the confessor chosen by him living too far for frequent oral confession.

power of teaching men to repent and to confess their sins.

A priest's ambition and love of power is constantly nourished by the honour and respect paid to him in virtue of his office. In honouring him, people honour, in the first instance, the Divine grace, and secondly, themselves as having recourse to this source of grace. It is an unforgivable error for a pastor to ascribe the honour to himself and feed his vanity upon it.* A priest used to occupying a place of honour and to having special attention paid to him may begin—if only inwardly—to seek and even to demand it. This of course means departing from Christ's way, and is a sign of the priest's fig-tree drying up. Envy is born of unsatisfied vanity and expresses itself in a lack of brotherly feeling for fellow-priests or even in finding fault with them, especially when their success as pastors is evident.

A priest's covetousness is often ascribed to the general materialistically-coloured background of clerical life. But in any case priests who do not vigorously resist this passion easily become "broken cisterns, that can hold no water" (JER. 2, 13).

---

* One famous preacher of Christ's truth was asked whether the respect paid to him by thousands of people does not trouble his mind. He answered: "Can the ass which carries the Lord and treads upon the garments spread in His way imagine that the joyous cries of the people are meant for it?"

14

Apologetics

THE ESSENCE of pastoral Orthodox apologetics is to reveal and expound Orthodoxy. The Lord's Word is not only Truth, but also Spirit and Life. In the same way Orthodoxy is not only truth, but also spirit and life. St. Paul in the second Epistle to the Corinthians (1, 20) says that the Lord Jesus Christ is "Yea" and "Amen,"— and the whole depth of the Orthodox apologetics as *positive* speech and action is expressed by these words.

A pastor who has preserved the spirit of the Chief Shepherd in himself and in his parish has done truly apologetical work, especially in our day when wolves of every kind make ample use of the smallest stain upon the Orthodox in order to estrange from Orthodoxy people who seek light.

We are convinced that when adequately revealed in life, Orthodoxy is an indestructible rock, not only in history, but in the human soul as well. It is the sharpest weapon against the world's unrighteousness, the most fragrant drink for those dying of thirst in its wilderness, the most healing remedy for all who have tasted suffering.

If the light of Christ is reflected in the pure mirror of

the soul, there appears the Light of Orthodoxy, the triumph of which the Church celebrates on the first Sunday in Lent. It is not accidental, of course, that this light shines forth after prayer and fasting.

If we contemplate the Gospel image of our Lord Jesus Christ we shall see *how* He spoke and *how* He was silent. We study Christ's words, but His silence is equally instructive. An apologist who knows how to keep silent knows the value of the true word and will never utter it in vain, or fill a vivid word with a colourless mental content.

An Orthodox apologist is a guardian not only of dogmatic symbols, but of spiritual life and faith. The Orthodox Creed is real only within the trinity of faith, life and spirit. Before taking part in a religious dispute about Truth or about certain aspects of it, an apologist must take stock not only of his ideas and knowledge but of his own spiritual condition as well. If his spirit is clouded with vanity, bitterness, irritability, pride, contempt for others (even if they be heretics), an Orthodox apologist cannot count himself worthy to come forth as a champion of Orthodoxy.

When approaching Truth, i.e. the Divine flame burning in the midst of a bush but not consuming it, an apologist 'puts his shoes from off his feet.' He puts off carnal feelings, thoughts and desires. Touching the flame of Truth, i.e. becoming a preacher of it, he burns with its fire everything in himself which is out of keeping with its spirit. Again, Truth is seen to be not only a 'two-edged sword' (REV. 1, 16) but a 'flaming sword' (GEN. 3, 24) which guards the way to Paradise — and the apologist becomes like an angel possessing the power to inspire and persuade.

Truth is imparted through testimony and inspiration. The soundest arguments and ideas remain dead and dry abstractions if they are not transmitted by a *living soul*—a witness to the Truth. This applies to preachers as well as to apologists. And a living soul is, first and foremost, a *loving* soul—one that loves man in spite of his errors and imperfections. Only such a soul has the right and the power to teach, to clarify, defend and transmit the Truth.

The Apostles had not only wisdom but love and spiritual power as well. The Lord Who is Love worked through them the same miracles of healing, renewing and raising to life as He had worked Himself. The Apostles not only persuaded men to accept the Truth, but by means of that Truth they actually freed their minds from falsehood. All that was left for man to do was to accept this liberation. Truth descended upon the hardened hearts and, like oil, softened them, opening them up. Truth warmed and enlightened the hearts of men.

"Now ye are clean through the word which I have spoken unto you" (JOHN 15, 3). Marvellous are the words of the Lord! We are accustomed to regard 'words' as something different from 'deeds.' And yet, a Divine word is at the same time a deed, and so is God's word which is spoken through man. This is how a true preacher and apologist is recognized.

Many 'weak' words are said in the world and in churches. They are 'weak' not because there are no profound ideas behind them—the ideas are sometimes quite subtle and eloquently expressed—but because there is no power of the spirit in them. That power is lacking in the men who utter them. One can only give what coins there are in one's purse. The spiritual purse filled with living Christian truth contains precious coins; but a purse filled with abstract thoughts, however profound and subtle, has only "sounding brass" in it.

People who seek real truth are not attracted to it by victorious disputations and wordy arguments. A person who is attracted by these is not a member of the Church.

An apologist must never pride himself on possessing the Truth — this is a very important feature of Orthodox apologetics. Truth must never belong to the apologist and thus be considered *his* truth. What is needed is that the erring soul should agree not with the human but with the Divine Truth, and then that Truth will be firmly established in it. Full agreement with the Truth is attained through the apologist's humility and his simple and straightforward attitude to people.

Some apologists are like the publican in the Gospel parable (these are of the apostolic type), and others like the Pharisee, priding themselves on their truth and making use of their 'rightness,' not in order to serve men but to dominate and look down upon them. Not infrequently 'Antisectarian' disputes were conducted in this spirit. Believers of every denomination felt broken-hearted after those meetings. Professional missionaries argued there with professional 'pundits'—Old Believers or 'Stundists.' People used 'the word of God' like a stick with which to beat one another.

We may and indeed we should meet people who interpret the Scriptures differently from us, or even follow a different path in their search for the primary Truth— God. But the Orthodox should always bring to such meetings the spirit of *goodwill to man,* regardless of how far the others at these meetings have strayed from Truth.

An Orthodox must feel confident that there is no need to defend the Truth of the Church of Christ—all that is necessary is *to reveal* it. It is the human soul that needs defending against its own errors, both voluntary and involuntary. A fire needs not defending but kindling; a blind man needs healing and not persuasion.

The signs of the Orthodox apologists are: to "heal the sick" (in mind), "cleanse the lepers" (in heart), "raise

70

the dead" (the spiritually dead), "cast out devils" (from their own and other people's souls). "Freely to give" (MATT. 10, 8) the Truth to men, without demanding any recognition of 'being in the right.' In the Truth the "great" is the servant of all.

These are the ways of the Kingdom of God appointed to the preachers and apologists of Orthodoxy.

15

Preaching

C AN TRUTH be proved? No. Truth cannot be proved; it can only be *proclaimed*. "How beautiful are the feet of them that preach the gospel of peace, and bring glad tidings of good things!" (ROM. 10, 15). First "peace," then "good things." Such is the path of an evangelist. All that is preceded by Christ's peace ("My peace I give unto you. . ."—JOHN 14, 27) brings *glad tidings* of the Divine Truth, a revelation of the heavenly reality.

A sermon is an outpouring of the Divine Spirit on the people, on their heart, mind and will. The woman in the parable put the leaven "in three measures of meal" (MATT. 13, 33).

A sermon may be prepared beforehand, or it may not be. If it is to be stronger than a double-edged sword (carrying Truth on one edge, and cutting down falsehood with the other), it must first of all be prepared in prayer. If the Spirit of power is given from above, the sermon will be 'a success' (i.e. will convince, inspire, heal, liberate, help the building of the Kingdom of God). If the spirit is not given, the sermon will either distract or weary the listeners.

Pastoral word has three forms: preaching—in church, lecturing—out of church, and bearing witness—in the homes (and in years of persecution — in the law courts). Each of these forms has its verbal limitations. Not all that can be said at home can be said in a lecture; not all that is said in a lecture should be said in church.

Sermons in church should not be unctuous, abounding in archaic words, and platitudes, and no artificial rhetorical devices are necessary. The preacher's words should be direct, simple, spiritually pure and have no 'worldly' taint about them (should not be borrowed from the newspapers).

To the pure every word is pure and harmless, but the reverent character of church worship and the language of the prayers create not only an inward state of reverence, but also its outer form, withdrawn from this world's vanity and leading to a higher, invisible realm. And it behoves the priest to guard this sense of reverence and not to disturb it by his words.

Only a man who is a true preacher in the home and under any circumstances can preach in church. A sermon which is not confirmed by the priest's life is like a picture of bread instead of real bread. There are *silent* pastors: their life speaks for them. Others say more by words than by the way they live. "There are diversities of gifts," and also of powers that give light to man and help him to soar. But blessed are those who do not 'strain at a gnat' in a pastor's life.

There are pastors who speak, and others who read their sermons. Those who cannot speak extempore, whose prayer for this gift has not been granted, have to read what they have written. And sometimes even those who can speak prefer to compose their sermon beforehand or to borrow it from another preacher. A priest is free in this matter, so long as his words, whether written or uttered at the inspiration of the moment are genuine and warm ("like freshly baked bread" as Fr. John of Kronstadt says), come from the heart, from the fulness of faith and the sweet desire to comfort, strengthen, enlighten and reassure.

A sermon can only strengthen and enlighten the listeners if it strengthens and enlightens the preacher himself. The angels of God "ascending and descending upon the Son of man" (JOHN 1, 51) stand by every devout priest and suggest the words to him, or if he reads words that have been written down, endow them with life-giving power.

"What you hear in the ear, that preach ye upon the housetops" (MATT. 10, 27). 'Ear' is the heart which is in touch with the invisible world. 'Housetop' is the pulpit, the reading desk, every place in the world. A pastor has a 'housetop'; in order to become a preacher he only needs a *heart that hears.*

16

The Prayer of St. Basil the Great

A PRIEST HAS TO STRUGGLE not with men, but with sin and with the incorporeal powers of evil. The Apostles wrestled against these powers and, clothed with the power of the Saviour, cast them out. The Lord bestows this power on the priests also: "Behold, I give unto you power to tread on serpents and scorpions, and over all the power of the enemy" (LUKE 10, 19). Serpents and scorpions are an exact image of the spiritual powers of evil — deadly poisonous and stealthily creeping in the dust (dealing with earthly values).

According to the prophecy of the book of Genesis, "the seed of the woman shall bruise the serpent's head" (GEN. 3, 15); but the serpent can 'bruise his heel.' In other words, there is left to the evil spirit the chance of externally harming the believers, of bringing men sorrow, disease, death, of raising clouds of passions and evil around them, and attempting to do it within them too. But everything that the world generally calls 'a misfortune' is merely a disease of 'the heel,' damage done to the temporary, shortlived human frame, restriction or even cessation of man's earthly existence only. The serpent cannot bruise a believer's 'head,' for his head is the Lord Jesus Christ in Whom and with Whom the fulness of a Christian's life is hid. "Your life is hid with Christ in God" (COL. 3, 3).

The enemy cannot worm itself into this holy of holies —into the will, heart and reason of a man who has ceased to live for himself and begun to live in Christ. "He that is begotten of God keepeth himself, and that wicked one toucheth him not" (I JOHN 5, 18).

The evil spirit finds his way into another region—the region of "the heel;" it attacks men (priests especially) in all the external circumstances of life, and even in the heart and mind—though not from within, but from outside, from "the heel." But a Christian is called to crush the reptile with his 'bruised heel,' despising its trifling bites and not allowing it to creep higher, i.e. to the region of the heart, the mind and the will.

In addition to guarding himself from the evil one, a pastor must guard his flock from him, encouraging his people in the struggle and instilling into them the conviction that the only sphere left to the devil is that of external circumstances and relations—"the heel" and that we must not fear those who 'kill the body' but cannot kill the soul. And indeed, whatever the evil one might do, whatever storms of calamity he might raise against individual men and mankind as a whole, he is powerless to make "the seed of the woman"—a believer—waver, or compel him to *side* with sin and rebel against God.

But the evil one tries to shake one's faith, so that having lost hope and love, a man should become the plaything of the dark, demonic waves that rage in the world; that he should no longer go up on those waves like Noah's ark but drown in them. A pastor is called to guard the existing faith and to implant it where it is absent—in both cases saving man from perdition and leading him into Life.

76

In sanctifying a man, the priest preserves him from the powers of evil and, as it were, *liberates his freedom* so that he may freely love God.

Many of little faith who, like Peter, have stepped onto the raging waves of the world's elements in order to go to Christ, become afraid and begin to sink. The waters of the world, the flesh and the devil, begin to rise above their 'heel'—the devil gains the power to torment their will and to force their heart. A priest can help such souls.*

A priest reads exorcisory prayers over them, gives them holy water, lets them kiss sacred objects. The Holy Eucharist is a great remedy and protection against the evil one and his works. Confession of the sins of a lifetime is of the utmost importance for a person who begins to suffer from demons.

A priest imparts to the sufferer from obsession the strength to struggle against demons, to disobey their suggestions, to despise them, to hate with holy evangelical hatred both them and sin through which they generally hold man in subjection. A priest teaches people to disbelieve demonic suggestions and slanders against God and men, to disregard the dark and evil thoughts which demons instill in their hearts and minds. *Rejected* thoughts and feelings will remain 'external' to us, beneath us, in the region of 'the heel.' But when demonic suggestions are accepted and approved of, they become seeds of evil in the soul and establish an organic link between it and the evil power.

Sometimes a man not only accepts, but nurtures the seed of evil by completely agreeing with it. He then becomes obviously possessed (though there are many who are possessed secretly).

A man tempted by an evil suggestion may be talked

---

* The true expression of pastoral power is to help.

out of it, persuaded to reject it, helped to repent of it. But a priest knows that it is impossible 'to persuade' the possessed or even the obsessed and that man himself suffers cruelly from the mad and blasphemous words which he utters and the actions he performs. The possessed must be helped.

Not every priest has the gracious power of immediately forbidding and banishing a demon from a man's soul and body. And there are different kinds of spirits: some may be soon driven away by the 'double-edged sword' of the pastor's faith and authority; others are more tenacious and must be methodically, patiently and firmly fought against by the power of the Lord given to the priest for this purpose.

It is necessary to use exorcisms. A demon is *tortured by them* and abandons its victim. Every Orthodox priest's Book of Offices contains the prayer of St. Basil the Great; in some books (e.g. those published by the Serbian Church) this prayer is considerably lengthened and a special rite of exorcising demons is drawn up — which is very appropriate for the time we live in.

An experienced priest will not be disconcerted by not seeing any immediate change in the possessed after the exorcism. An exorcism pronounced firmly, courageously, from the heart, with complete faith and righteous indignation against the demons, *always* has effect, but sometimes the effect is not noticeable at once.

Exorcisory prayer is torture for the demon, who generally shows this while the prayer is recited. The patient becomes inordinately excited, shouts, gesticulates.

There are various forms of obsession; it is a subject that requires special study. For our present purpose it is sufficient to say that 'possession' indicates the state of a soul entirely dominated by a demon (or several demons), so that all consciousness of self is lost. A man's personality is completely enslaved. In the case of 'obsession' the soul or the body is only partly dominated by an evil power. The obsessed retains self-consciousness to the full and is able to pass moral judgment on his actions, but has no power to struggle against the obsession.

Ninty percent of suicides take their last step under the direct influence of spirits which are "murderers from the beginning" (JOHN 8, 44). And properly speaking almost every suicide is murder committed by a demon through the instrumentality of the man himself.

Many a pastor is responsible for having failed to protect those unfortunate sheep of his flock snatched away by the invisible destroyer.

A priest is truly able 'to tread over all the power of the enemy' which surrounds him or which enslaves and destroys another person. He must rescue the sheep from the wolves, both "intellectual" wolves in the flesh and incorporeal ones.

A pastor's whole life and service is a means of rescuing the sheep. But a special means—which some pastors mistakenly neglect—is the exorcisory prayer.

17

Eucharist

THE PRIEST'S CALLING is to offer thanks . . . especially in our days of murmuring, 'distress of nations' and perplexity (LUKE 21, 25). The sacrament of the Eucharist—the crown of pastoral service—is in itself a thanksgiving. The priest offers thanks for himself, for all who are praying—and for those who have not as yet learned to pray. He gives thanks for our life and for everything as he lifts the Holy Chalice: "Bringing before Thee thine of thine own in all and for all. . . ." A priest's whole life is as it were the lifting of this Cup to the Lord—His Cup— to Him, which is the greatest possible human expression of gratitude and love.

The congregation takes part in the holy thanksgiving by partaking of the Holy Mysteries and by eating the blessed Antidoron after devoutly attending to the Liturgy.

A priest does right in encouraging the laity to approach the Holy Chalice. Frequent communion may be unadvisable for some, but the number of parishioners who have to be restrained from communion is always smaller than those who have to be urged to come. It should be a pastor's continual practice to draw more and more people to commune increasingly more often. Through confession and getting to know his parishioners in their homes he will easily notice those who especially need strengthening with the Holy Gifts. They may be sinful, but sincerely struggling against their sinfulness, or they may be people who are particularly subject to attacks of the evil spirit. Holy Communion is needed by such men above all. For to those who have learned to govern their passions Holy Communion is necessary as a gracious means of safe-guarding their spiritual freedom and making them love God more fervently. A priest who knows by experience the healing power of the holy sacrament of the Body and Blood will never venture to withhold this great gift of God from sinful people for whose sake this gift came down from heaven.

Of course there may be cases of people coming to Christ's Mysteries unworthily, without penitence, without a decision to forsake sin or a genuine desire to struggle against it.* In such cases a pastor must be firm in defending the Holy Mysteries from the Judas kiss of the human soul, and in guarding that soul itself from the terrible Flame of the sacrament. But it is essential for every priest to cultivate the Eucharistic life in his parish. And if on a Sunday when the Holy Gifts are brought out and it is said, "With faith and in the fear of God draw near," there are no communicants in the parish—does not the whole congregation appear to be excommunicated?

---

* Strange as it seems, such cases are most frequent in Lent, because some people communicate only at that season simply from habit 'fulfilling their duty'—a sad inheritance from the past.

18

Material Problems

FROM THE POINT OF VIEW of the Christian faith, this is a simple matter; from the point of view of 'pastoral purity' and modern church psychology it is a painful subject. A man conscious of himself as a soldier of Christ will not involve himself in 'buying or selling;' he will strive to be as unencumbered as possible both with regard to his needs and to his requirements. Love will do the rest: love for a pastor who is not self-seeking and who is of spiritual value to his parishioners will supply him with all that is necessary, and the pastor's love for his flock will be a secure foundation of its love for him.

The best, and indeed the only, solution to the problem is for the parishioners to make monthly contributions toward providing a modest livelihood for their preist, doing this with a loving, filial consideration for his needs.

In truth, and in accordance with "inward" justice, a parish which is not prepared to share *its last* with it's pastor, so that undistracted by material cares he may devote himself entirely to his work, is not worthy to have a pastor at all. "If we have sown unto you spiritual things, is it a great thing if we shall reap your carnal things?" (I COR. 9, 11).

19

Relations with the Parish

THE PARISH CONSTITUTION of 1918 was introduced in the Russian Church for regulating the relations between the pastor and his parishioners. But *right* relations are not and cannot be regulated by law. If there is a question of 'lawful demands' and 'claiming one's rights', that means absence of true church life, for the sake of which churches are built and pastors exist.

In Parish relations formalism must be replaced by 'family spirit,' by a reverent, spiritual intimacy between the priest, the church-warden, the members of the parish council and so on. The church-warden must be, and be conscious of being, a 'deacon' in the early apostolic sense of the term, one who 'serves tables' (ACTS 6, 2), i.e. one who looks after the material interests of the church community. Like the priest, he is the servant of the parish, though his task is different. But the church-warden must always remember to put the care about 'the tables' in the second place: his first care, like the priest's, must be *service to the human soul*. Rudeness, lack of delicacy, "bossiness" in church as though it belonged to him, are criminal in a church-warden; this sinful attitude toward their work on the part of church-wardens was developed by the system of electing rich men to the post without considering their spiritual suitability for it. This must no longer be done.

The parish priest's co-workers should be devout, spiritually zealous people—this is the chief point to take into consideration when electing church-wardens or members of the parish council; their business efficiency is a secondary consideration. The parish may lose this or that material advantage, but it will be free from the demonic spirit of ambition, vanity, dissension and pride.

The pastor, the church-warden, the members of the parish council should be like a closely knit family, completely trusting one another and united by the same purpose—to bring holiness into men's lives.

20

Missionary Work

ONE OF THE SIGNS of a parish being truly Orthodox is its proselytising activity—an apostolic zeal to attract new souls to the faith. Almost all parishes strive to acquire new members in a purely external sense, but few attract people to the church for their own sake and not for the sake of their subscriptions. "I seek not yours, but you" (II COR. 12, 14) said St. Paul to those to whom he preached the Gospel. Orthodox parishes, likewise, must seek not people's possessions, but the people themselves.

Instead of unnecessary conversations about purely material subjects and financial projects, parish councils might give a part of their time to discussing the most essential work of the Church—attracting new souls to the faith.

In addition to the priest's work in this field, all parish workers must take part in missionary activities: arranging lectures, not only for the parish but for 'outsiders' as well; printing weekly or monthly leaflets—religious, educative and apologetical; founding a parish reading room and library of religious books approved by the pastor; and subscribing to religious periodicals.

Members of the parish who collect monthly subscriptions must be secret *missionaries*. This is the main feature of their work and of their search for new members. Coming into touch with people who voluntarily* give their mite for the support of the church and parish priest, the collectors—sensitive and believing Christians—must establish spiritual contact with them and feel responsible for drawing them closer and closer to the Church.

When attracting new members to the parish and asking them to give it material help, the collectors must always emphasize that this help is entirely free and voluntary, and is of value only in so far as it comes from the heart.

As representatives of the Church who come to strange houses on its behalf and not for personal reasons, the collectors must know how to answer, gently and in the spirit of love this or that question about the Orthodox faith, the Church, the services; when collecting subscriptions, they must distribute (freely, of course) religious literature, leaflets, etc., and bring copies of the Gospel. They must tell the priest about this unofficial missionary work and indicate to him people who are particularly in need of his visits.†

A parish that strives for such activity, for such true understanding of the purpose and meaning of the earthly Church's existence will be a true blessing for the world around it.

Souls that have grown cold and gone astray in the world can only be drawn to God through a gracious understanding and fulfilment of His work on earth.

---

* Contributions must always be voluntary, in no way binding, and must on no account be a *condition* for entering a parish.

† In some parishes not only the pastor's closest co-workers, but ordinary parishioners as well take part in attracting to the Church unbelievers and those of little faith.

21

The Spirit of Parish Management

PARISH LIFE is a ladder to the Kingdom of God—it trains our thoughts, feelings and wills for that Kingdom and teaches us its meaning.

All that lives upon earth is subject, in its measure, to the earthly laws of life, and even the holiest thing on earth—the Church of Christ—is not free from the burden of the world's material relations. The Apostles surrounding their Divine Master Who could change water into wine and multiply bread carried with them nevertheless a bag into which people put alms to support them and supply the needs of the Lord Himself. There was no sin in this; it was in keeping with the laws of fallen man's material existence, and at the same time it called forth exalted feelings of love, mercy and sacrifice in the people to whom these feelings were preached.

But the man who carried the bag was infected with the spirit of materialism, greed and miserliness; he grudged the fragrant ointment for the Saviour of the world, and perished a traitor. He was not faithful in that which is least, and proved to be unfaithful also in much. This is an instructive example for us: everyone who becomes attached to money will betray Christ the Saviour. The Christian's attitude toward money must be sober, free, light, without any heart-felt attachment. One must not be unreasonably attached to earthly life as a whole, and still less so to its values taken in isolation, especially to material ones. Only a soul free from materialism can truly have faith, and when its hour comes, pass over to the other world unperturbed.

Material things for church use are quite legitimately sold in the porch (a place symbolizing the outer court of the tabernacle) *for the believers' convenience,* since it would be more difficult for them to buy votive candles or the bread of offering elsewhere. But it must be clearly felt and understood that all material transactions of the Church, as well as all its spiritual experiences, are free and voluntary. Union in the parish, understood as union in the incipient Kingdom of God, has nothing compulsory about it and is entirely voluntary. Every believer determines for himself the amount of his subscription to the church funds and pays it without being urged to do so. Objects of material value, like candles and prosphoras, are bought voluntarily. The collection plate is passed around, attracting only the willing hand. And everything which concerns prayer must be on an equally clear and purely voluntary basis.

It is usual to pay for special services. But not everyone is aware that this is a *donation on the occasion of a special service,* and not a payment for it. It is impossible 'to pay' for a church service, since every such service is valid only through the presence in it of the Holy Spirit, and the Spirit of God cannot be given or received at any cost, but descends upon men only in answer to disinterested prayer, faith and love. A true special Office is infinitely more precious than any material payment offered for it, were it equal to all the world's treasures.

And, *vice versa,* a false, hypocritical special Office is utterly worthless and indeed is a sin in the sight of God, both for the layman and, still more so, for the priest.

How can one price a priest's blessing which has given the grace of peace and health and repelled the evil spirit? Obviously, it is a Divine *gift* and, like every prayer, can only be regarded as a gift, since, in the words of St. Paul, "the Spirit itself maketh intercession for us with groanings which cannot be uttered" (ROM. 8, 26).

Every attempt to buy the Spirit or to pay for it is doomed not merely to failure, but to an utter rejection of it by God. It is sufficient to recall Simon Magus (ACTS 8, 18-23) who wanted to pay the Apostles for grace— and their answer to him.

Therefore it is essential always clearly to distinguish between 1) prayer, sacrament, blessing, i.e. "church offices" (the need of the Spirit) and 2) gifts of money, in connection with this need.

Since a request or a thanksgiving sometimes involves bodily privations (fasting, almsgiving, a vow, as means of softening and humbling the spirit), there grew up a habit of associating and, indeed, inseparably connecting the material sacrifice with church prayer. And this habit immediately became in the eyes of materialistically-minded people "payment for a special office," supposed to be invariably attached to it. And later on it was directly said that payment for a special service is legitimate payment to the priest and the reader for their "labours"— as though prayer were work like any other. This was in itself a sign of spiritual deterioration of the church community. In apostolic times and at the best periods of Church history the believers thought differently. They supported the priest's material life for his service as a whole, but introduced no tax for special prayers.

Pastoral and prayerful service is not ordinary work; it is *service to God* — Divine service. Even the least service to God is a reward in itself for the celebrant and the most perfect payment for the work which this service involves. The work of the priest and of every Church server is the angelic work of building up the Heavenly Church.

A Christian's, and especially a pastor's spiritual food is to do the will of Him Who sent us into the world. The soul cannot be offered a material reward for taking this sweet food. Prayer is a man's spiritual nourishment, a precious jewel of the soul, and cannot be paid for in perishable earthly values. Otherwise we shall have nothing but those values left us, as indeed we already see it happening: the buyers and sellers are left with their cankered treasure, their hearts failing them for looking after the terrible catastrophes that are coming on the earth. Within church precincts a struggle must be waged against militant materialism, not by words only, but by actions.

22

A Life of Prayer

A PRIEST'S LIFE begins with prayer, and ends on earth with prayer too—in order to begin again with prayer in heaven.

The first sign of devoutness is *composure,* the positive power of self-limitation in the external world, the "narrow" (i. e. the straight, the shortest) way of following the Lord — the way "which leadeth unto life."

The second sign is *continence* ("against such there is no law" — GAL. 5, 23). A pastor must be *light,* unburdened, so that he may be always prayerful. One who cultivates the spiritual "breathing of the heart" will never neglect the weapon of continence.

The third sign: a reverent way of making the sign of the cross. A priest should always give his blessing attentively, not haphazardly, not carelessly, not in the middle of a joke. A reverently made sign of the cross has great power.

The fourth sign: not taking the name of the Lord in vain. The name of God, the Name which moves the world, the Name "above all other names" which is the joyful tremor of angels (and of righteous priests) and the flame consuming the powers of darkness—this Name must not be pronounced 'from habit' — without prayer, without a tremor.

Continual inward prayer is the condition of pastoral power. The priest is called to surround with the breath of prayer everyone who comes to him, invisibly for that person but visibly for God and the angels who rejoice at this prayer, and sensibly for the powers of evil who are scorched by it. A vigilant pastor will not miss a single contact with a person without saying this inward prayer for him and, if occasion permits, saying a few words "seasoned with salt." This constructive work is the essence of pastorship.

Church life deteriorates chiefly because pastors pronounce a number of insipid, spiritually saltless words and become so used to them that when later on they want to say some "seasoned" words — they cannot: the words sound unnatural, abstract, false and didactic, and are powerless to regenerate a soul. But a pastor who guards his lips from this world's insipidity, by doing so enters the realm of inward prayer, and the prayer itself guards his lips and heart from devastation.

"He that believeth on Me, as the Scripture hath said, out of his belly shall flow rivers of living water" (JOHN 7, 38). A spiritually-minded priest is a source of living water for souls who seek not abstract, moral or dogmatic teaching, but a revelation of the reality of faith. This heavenly reality reveals itself not only in prayer or preaching but in all the words and actions of a spiritually-minded man, and when seen as a part of everyday life, it is particularly irresistible.

A true priest is 'collected,' constantly vigilant in prayer, and he 'seasons' the world with his whole life, with all his words and actions—voluntary and, especially, involuntary.

He knows his tree "by its fruits" (MATT. 7, 16). The fruits of pastoral labor appear first of all in the pastor's own heart. For "the husbandman that laboreth must be first partaker of the fruits" (II TIM. 2, 6).

23

Death

A PRIEST'S DEAD BODY is not washed by anyone. No one of his sons must see his father's nakedness. His fellow priests come, and wiping the flesh with pure oil, array the body in the priestly vestments. They cover the face with an aer, so that it will be covered like that of Moses whose face shone with an intolerable light after he had seen God. The Gospel which the pastor had served while on earth is put into his hands.

When laymen are buried, one lesson from the Gospel is read; at a priest's burial — five. Instead of the Psalms, the Gospel is read over the priest's body. The Gospel was the heart of his life and it has a central part at his burial.

The canon of the sixth Tone: "In the waves of the sea" is sung — the same that is sung over the Sepulchre before the Easter matins, when the moments of waiting for the Resurrection pass so slowly and tremulously.

He is departed. Moses the pastor has gone up into the Mount and beholds his Lord. And those who are left at the foot of the Mount of Life sing:

"Thy godly minister, made a partaker of the nature Divine in his Translation hence, through Thy life-giving mystery, O Christ, is now come unto Thee.

"Receive Thou his soul in Thy hand, as it were a bird, O Saviour. Establish Thou him in Thy courts, and in the choir of the Angels; and because of Thy great mercy, O Lord, give rest unto him whom Thou hast taken by Thy command.

"Strange is the mystery of death: for it cometh to all untimely. Nature is dissolved by force. It taketh old men, abbots and learned men; it slayeth the teachers of vain philosophies, bishops and pastors, and every nature of mortals. But let us cry aloud with tears: Because of Thy great mercy, O Lord, give rest unto him whom Thou hast taken by Thy command.

"He who lived in godliness, and was adorned as Thy priest, the sacrificer and minister of Thy divine mysteries, by Thy divine command hath passed over from life's clamor unto Thee. Save him, whom as priest, Thou didst accept, O Savior; and because of Thy great mercy, give him rest with the just."*

---

* Quoted from Isabel Hapgood's translation.

PART TWO

1

Welfare and Poverty

THE POOR may enrich the rich. The rich may im-
poverish the poor. What different sense is given to
these words by the world! Unbelievers mean by them
that the rich exploit the poor. Those who believe in
Christ and live in Him see in them a far deeper and
wider meaning: a materially poor man may uplift and
spiritually enrich by the purity and loftiness of his spirit
those who are materially richer than himself. And *vice
versa*, a rich man morally gone astray certainly spiritually
"impoverishes" the poor who come into contact with
him. For not only is everyone 'responsible for all,' but
everyone, whatever his social position, *influences* everyone else. People's moral and spiritual energies continu-
ally, though invisibly to the superficial eye, go like waves
over the world, meeting one another, so that individuals
act as factories of good and evil, as conductors of Christ's
light, or of darkness — not only for themselves but for
the world as a whole.

Material wealth is not in itself pernicious (it is morally neutral), and material poverty is not in itself useful

for uplifting the soul (it too is morally neutral). But the lust of wealth and its deification is poison both for individuals and society: it means that human sacrifices are made to wealth (and the foolish rich sacrifice to it both themselves and those around them) and that the purpose of man's life and his great and immortal dignity are forgotten. The lust of wealth is found not only among the rich and prosperous but quite frequently among the poor who *envy* other people in their material prosperity. The essence of Christian spirit is freedom from all attachment to perishable wealth, and every man, whatever his social position, may be liberated in Christ and become free in spirit from selfish avarice and envy.

Poverty that breathes of murder and lives by envy is not the blessed poverty of the Gospel. It is a horrible poverty. On the other hand, the humble rich who regard themselves merely as 'stewards' (LUKE 16) of the wealth which belongs to the Creator and *justly* administer it, entering through it into a *merciful relation to the world* certainly cannot be numbered among the rich to whom the Saviour said 'Woe!' No, not woe but joy, joy everlasting, to *such* rich!

Nothing material and no absence of anything material is in itself either good or evil. Only Marxism, following in the steps of Buddhism (strange as this sounds), raises the material side of existence into a moral category of good and evil (thus manifesting the essentially religious, though negative, character of its teaching). For Christians nothing external is either good or evil, but everything in the world becomes good or evil through man's inner motives and intentions. Both good and evil are purely inward, spiritual states which create either hell or paradise within man. The external world is merely the periphery of man's manifestations, and of course if the man himself be full of light, the periphery of his life will give out light also.

It was not material riches as such that the Saviour called evil, but 'trusting in riches,' i.e. building one's life upon the idea of material welfare. The instability and insecurity of such riches and such trust is emphasized in the Gospel in every way. It is "the house built upon sand" and "the rich man who fared sumptuously every day" and did not understand that sudden death lay in wait for him. The Revelation very definitely says of such riches: "thou sayest, I am rich and increased with goods, and have need of nothing; and knowest not that thou art wretched and miserable and poor and blind and naked" (REV. 3, 17). In the reverse sense these words might be applied to a materially poor man rich in good and lofty feelings and self-sacrificing actions, but conscious only of his poverty and his earthly insignificance: "thou sayest thou art poor, and wretched and miserable, hast need of everything, but knowest not that thou art rich in Christ, rich in eternity, and no one can rob thee of this wealth which gives thee everlasting bliss. . . ."

If all men were thoroughly imbued with this true vision of reality, how different their life would be! All the horrible theories breathing of hate that replace one another in the world would vanish, and the true, right attitude to earthly values would be established. Those earthly values, no longer regarded as supreme, would become *real*.

Wealth may be God's blessed gift — and so may poverty. Wealth may be a curse — and so may poverty. Poverty becomes accursed when it is *proletarized*. Wealth is accursed when it proletarizes the poor. To proletarize poverty is to deprive of blessing the souls of the poor — to deprive them of the spiritual means of acquiring and retaining that blessing; it is also to *isolate and exclude*

the poor because they are poor. To cultivate such prole-
tarization means spiritually to destroy the poor — which
is the task of non-religious socialism culminating in
Marxism; it means instilling the spirit of antichrist into
the poor. Of course this process had not begun with
Karl Marx or the leaders of early socialism. It is simply
a manifestation of *sin in the world* — both in the world
of the rich and of the poor. A poor man 'proletarizes'
poverty by his wrong attitude toward it, and a rich man
does the same thing by his wrong attitude toward his own
wealth and toward the poverty of others, and thus heaps
coals of fire on his head. To a believing Christian it is
perfectly obvious that the godless attitude to life widely
prevalent in the modern capitalistic world is as much an
evil as the atheistic proletarian revolution.

At the present time Christian consciousness — truly
Orthodox Christian consciousness, in whomsoever it may
be manifested — must enter the path of ideological and,
what's more, of spiritual activity against the proletariza-
tion of poverty both by the poor and by the rich. That
activity must be a sacred struggle for the greatest value
in the world — the soul of man — and be waged only
through the living human personality, through the union
of those who are *living in Christ* and can affirm by their
own example the principles which they profess.

The world is not divided into two camps — capitalists
and proletarians, as it appears to superficial observation.
There are *three* camps in the world: 1) godless poor; 2)
godless rich; and 3) materially poor and rich Christians.
This is how the world is morally mapped out. Christians
are not divided into 'rich' and 'poor,' for the poor are
aware of the advantages of their poverty and the rich of
the impediment of their wealth, or in any case of its insecurity and therefore — insignificance. And all follow
their own path, perform their own *service.* It is only for

this third group that there can be a 'social problem' in the proper sense. For the first two it does not and cannot exist, for they are actuated by the principle of struggle and irreconcilable discord, so that for them there is either war or purely diplomatic and unreal peace. The third group is of course the smallest in the world, for the heavenly and honorable privilege of belonging to it is derived not from verbal professions or even ideological beliefs (this should be emphasized) but from actual, spiritually real Christian faith. It is only this spiritual reality that can give rise to the true conception of Christian social life.

A Christian is one who *labors* whether he is rich or poor. Whatever his social and material position may be, a Christian is a laborer in the field of life. By the sweat of his brow he earns his physical and also his spiritual bread: eternal life in Christ. "If any would not work, neither should he eat," says St. Paul (II THESS. 3, 10), and his words are a Divine commandment to all Christians. If a man has material bread without having to work for it or to struggle with earth's thorns and thistles (for instance, if he has investments) he does not, if he is a Christian, remain idle, but procures bread for others and thus acquires spiritual bread both for himself and for others. A Christian who has property is never idle, but always 'labors'. And if he does not labor, he is not a Christian.

This is why all Christians are in the same camp — rich and poor, distinguished and insignificant—according to earthly standards; and it is bound to be so. Christians are free both from envy and from contempt. The exalted and the lowly know themselves to be equal on the plane of eternity, and therefore there can be no envy for the exalted or contempt for the lowly. In proportion to his labor and in accordance with God's will (apart from which nothing happens either in heaven or on earth) a

Christian reaches this or that material position, which is *the most useful and salutary for him.*

The passions of men who have lost their Divine likeness may rage around him; others may try to entice him into this or that human camp welded together not by love but by solidarity in pursuing low and often criminal ends. A Christian will not sell his world-transcending, spiritual freedom for the mess of red pottage which the transitory world offers him—and he will not build his happiness upon the suffering of others.

For the Church of Christ "there are no rich and no poor. . ." or, rather, there are, but on a different plane. Wealth and poverty have a different quality in the Church. "The rich" are *the poor in spirit;* "the poor" are those who deem themselves rich because of their earthly poverty. It is the practice of the Church with regard to the rich that they should *serve Her,* and with regard to the poor that She should serve *them.* Thus the poor are regarded as worthy of help, and the rich are worthy of serving. The psychology of the Church is directly opposed to the one prevalent in the world, where the poor serve, and the rich accept this service as their due. It is noteworthy that the same law of the Church is observed even beyond the boundaries of the earth: the departed saints pray for sinful men in this world and thus further their salvation; believers still living on earth, being richer than the departed sinners who lost their opportunity of doing good on earth, can help them by their prayers and thus further their salvation.

In this spiritual sense service is preeminently the work of 'the rich'; and in the earthly sense, too, wealth, power, position are always connected for the Christian mind with the idea of *service* and certainty, not with greater enjoyment of the earthly life (that is a pagan principle, and indeed even paganism in its higher forms rose above this Epicurian attitude).

101

The Church on earth and in heaven is essentially the servant of all the "least," the helpless, the oppressed, the needy (whether in the earthly or in the spiritual sense). "The strong ought to bear the infirmities of the weak and not to please themselves" (St. Paul's commandment). This is why the Church stoops to heal, equally, the rich and the poor: the rich who 'trust in riches' and the poor grieving over their poverty and sick with envy toward the rich.

This is why true servitors of the Church never fawn on the rich, even if the rich give money to the Church and build temples for it. The servitors of the Church are impartial both to wealth and to poverty, and do not fall into the other extreme — that of denouncing wealth *as such*. The Church knows that men shall be judged not according to their external position, but according to the purity of their hearts and the degree of their love for God and man — love expressed by their deeds.

Modern godless communists demoralize the poor, segregating them into a class by themselves and making them wage a deadly struggle against another class, "the rich;" they unbridle the lower instincts and rouse murderous hatred and envy. The godless rich have no consideration and never have had for the poor as *human beings*. They only yield to the material pressure of the poor. By their hard-heartedness and by clinging to their 'cankered' riches (JAMES 5, 2) they unbridle — just as godless communists do — the lower instincts of the poor, for in their selfishness they show themselves to be apostles of atheism. And those representatives of the Church who were not true to its spirit frequently *demoralized the rich* by fawning upon them, countenancing their hypocriscy, passing over in silence their misdeeds. And of course we too, representatives of the great

102

Russian Church, have been guilty of it. We have not been able to win the spiritual confidence of the Russian masses and most of them have deserted us. We have not shown spiritual impartiality or cared sufficiently for the souls of the Russian people, both poor and rich. There can be no restoration, no renaissance of our Orthodox Russian culture until we have passed through the cleansing fire of penitence and recognized our mistakes and sins. The clergy must show an example not only of service, but also of penitence.

On the paths of our own history we must be convinced of the *righteousness* of God's Judgment upon us, and woe to those of us who will find that judgment "undeserved!"

"Even so, Lord God Almighty, true and righteous are Thy judgments" (Rev. 16, 7).

2

Philosophy of Ownership

1. MAN CAN ONLY POSSESS that which belongs to God. The world is God's creation and so is man. Man can in no way escape from God's ownership. To whatever heights he may ascend — everywhere there is God's ownership, infinite, inconceivable, unfathomable. Pilate sinks to the depths of treachery: he is ready to give the Innocent Sufferer to be crucified. And what does he hear from the Divine Wisdom? "Thou couldest have no power at all against me, except it were given thee from above" (JOHN 19, 11). Uniting in Himself and in all His words the fullness of the earthly and the heavenly, the Saviour recalled to Pilate both the Caesars from whom he received his power and also the Source of *all* power and ownership.

2. One may *conceal* oneself from God, from the sight of the Lord. Thus Adam hid in the bushes, concealing himself from God. This is the naive psychology of every sinner. "Adam, where art thou?"....."I hid myself...." Numberless years have passed since then, and the sons of Adam still imagine that they can

hide from God. And they do 'hide' as best they can: in the overgrown and tangled ideological thickets of this world's culture — 'private property,' 'public property,' 'state property,' 'communism,' 'capitalism,' 'socialism,' 'freedom,' 'slavery,' 'wealth,' 'poverty,' 'possessions,' 'economic laws' and so on, and so on.

3. At the base of everything complex there must be simplicity. If this primary simplicity is absent, there is chaos instead of complexity. But if the fundamental simplicity is present, the complexity will be a harmony. It is only in the light of the knowledge of the primary laws of life laid down by the Creator that our complex secular culture can come to resemble a harmonious orchestra in which there are no superfluous instruments.

It is only through the knowledge of these *absolute* laws that we can estimate all human conceptions and determine their true significance. The world always has belonged and will belong to God alone, whatever forces may be temporary masters of it.

But does this mean that man has not and cannot have any property whatever? On the contrary, human property has its firm basis in the fact that there is property as such, and that there is a Master of it all. And if there is a true Master, that means property may be *given*. What a broad and deep basis for all true possession! In view of *this* basis it becomes comprehensible why one must not steal, must not appropriate anything, must not 'grow rich' and exalt oneself through anything. All property belongs to God, just as life belongs to Him. And He gives property, just as He gives life.

4. Man is given 'a talent' — a span of physical life, of mental faculties, of spiritual possibilities. It is given not for burying in the ground, but for cultivating.

105

The whole span of a man's life may be compared to a plot of ground. His duty is not idly to lie on this God-given ground but to cultivate it, to make the most of the life given into his stewardship as a token of a better life, better soil. "He that is faithful in that which is least is faithful also in much." Only that which is 'least' is given to man. However great in his earthly eyes this 'least' may seem, it is very small by comparison with that which it prefigures. But even this 'least' must be put to use for the benefit of the world. This is why rich people who make creative use of their wealth, while living humbly, are true Christians in spite of their "great possessions."

"Mine is only that which I gave away," said St. Maxim the Confessor. Gave . . . to whom? To God, to men. . . . There are people who make no use of their wealth. Among them there are some who have 'hidden it for themselves,' buried it in the ground, and there are some who have given it to God, believing that their duty is merely to distribute it in the world as justly as possible. This gracious *stewardship* of wealth finds different expressions. Some give their wealth away at once or by degrees. Others retain all the appearance of possession, but in their heart sincerely surrender it to God, so that their task is merely a fair distribution of it. It may take the form of ordinary economic enterprise, of a good industrial or agricultural business. *In appearance* it will be like all the works 'of this world,' but in its inner content it will already be a small realization of the Kingdom of God.

Thus A. S. Khomiakov had land and serfs, and yet at bottom he was not his serfs' owner but rather their solicitous father and indeed their servant. This is the psychology of all wealthy Christians: landowners, industrialists, factory owners. . . . This too was the attitude of truly Orthodox tsars.

When the Lord Jesus Christ said, "He that is greatest among you shall be your servant," he meant by 'greatest' him who is rich, whether in money, or in rank, or in talent. . . ."The greatest" must *serve* and not exercise power through the gifts (material or spiritual) which have been entrusted to him *for a time only*.

5. All *earthly* possessions are shortlived and "full of trouble," for no sooner do they come and man gets attached to them than they disappear, abandoning him to perplexity, pain, sorrow and death. They leave emptiness in their place, and dust in the place of man. But until possessions are replaced by emptiness they can bear "much fruit," even small possessions of the poor: the widow's mite proved to be a greater value, a greater force for good than the treasures of the Pharisees.

6. A man has less property than he thinks. It is only in his imagination that a millionaire owns his millions — in truth they own him. For the most part he is fettered by them, compelled to a certain style of living, bound up with a particular set of people, inevitably surrounded by flattery, envy, insincerity, obsequiousness, solicitations, attempts on his life — physical and mental. Is not this slavery, penal servitude, increasing in severity with the increase in wealth? Does that which can be bought for money amount to much? Can *spiritual peace*—the highest happiness —be bought?

7. But from another point of view a man's possessions are *far greater than he thinks*. Every breath of air which gets into his lungs is his property, far more so than a coin in his pocket, for it directly supports his

life. Every ray of sunshine that warms a man is *his* warmth, wholly united to him. And so in everything, in the smallest manifestations of life man is surrounded with *property*, with God's gifts poured upon him and transmuted into his very life. Great and glorious is this law which makes every man rich.

8. In order to enter into the harmony of the world that became discordant but is now being tuned up again, a man must in all conscience (and not merely with his intellect) recognize God's power and himself become God's property, since the universe is already His property. Numberless myriads of worlds, suns, stars and innumerable septillions of lives move within the limits laid down by the Creator. Stones, water, air, earth, fire, obey immutable laws which man may detect, which are for him 'to discover.' What for? For the sake of learning how to live in accordance with these laws. Submission to physical laws is only a symbol of submission to God's spiritual laws. Just as physical nature reveals itself to man in natural science, physics, chemistry, mechanics, cosmography and so on, so spiritual nature is revealed in the Gospel. Observing the subordination of physical nature to God, man must learn to subordinate his spirit to Him.

9. A sober-minded and unprejudiced man naturally thinks and sees that his earthly possessions are no more than 'relative.' Centuries melt away and so does all human property on earth. All earthly 'rights' of individuals, cities and nations — the right to own land and goods, even the right to live — disappear into thin air.

The only thing indestructible in the universe is the Divine power which creates the worlds. All else is fragile and destructible. *And it is destructible simply in order that men should not regard the destructible as indestructible*. In the life of the world to come, when "the wheat is gathered," i.e. when men who were righteous and loved God will be gathered from all the ages — no one will be in danger of loving the creature more than the Creator, and then once more, as in Paradise, *the destructible will become indestructible*. But no one will defy the eternal and indestructible nature. All will contemplate the glory of God alone and in its unutterable light see the whole of existence and find their undying life eternally renewed.

10. This state is impossible for us on earth, for we are all the time loving someone or something more than God. Our heart is 'adulterous' in the deepest, religious sense of the word. This is why the Saviour (Who never spoke unjustly) called men "an *adulterous* and sinful generation." Fallen humanity is attached to transitory values, cleaves to the pleasures of this world, to its illusory wealth and its equally illusory glory. If it were not for worms, rust, moth, locusts, stench, corruption, suffering and death, the world would be *a living hell*. Some people fancy that the reverse is true: if there were no pain and sorrow on this earth, it would be 'paradise.' But *it would be hell*. The sinfulness of earthly flesh is covered by earthly sorrows. The blessed salt of suffering preserves the human spirit from decay and eternal death. It preserves it in people who understand and accept Christ's 'narrow way.'

    This is why for the righteous *all the ways of the Lord* are blessed, "true and righteous altogether." This is why the Cross of every life lived on this transitory earth is *blessed*.

11. Human life finds its highest expression in complete devotion to God. As man is freed from "the pride of

life, the lust of the flesh and the lust of the eyes" (from materialism of every sort) he becomes more and more 'transparent to God, so that the all-pure Spirit of God may dwell in him. And when man is completely transparent, free from all pride, from all sinful fondness for himself and the world, God's property — the world — will become his property, and 'having nothing' and not even belonging to himself, he will "possess all things," as St. Paul says (II Cor. 6, 16). God will abide in man and will make his life rich and restful. This serene harmony of life is the Kingdom of God.

12. The sequence of temporal life is given to man as a ladder for ascending to eternal life. Only he who is faithful "in that which is least (the temporal) is faithful also in much (the eternal)." While we are still here on earth we must learn to live the eternal life. Those who are not grafted to God's Vine (John 15, 5) cannot live. Mounting the ladder of earthly life and earthly values (i.e. drawing away from them) we enter into the Kingdom of God. But if a man draws away from the values of the world *in a wrong direction* (e.g. a despairing man, a suicide), he falls into an abyss.

13. The material world is a 'staff' for the sick soul, its anchor, the point of application of the primary forces of the spirit — a staff which helps us to ascend to God, if we know how to use it. Everything in the world is created or is permitted for man's benefit, and he can convert even the most trying and painful manifestations of earthly life (sometimes, indeed, better than any other) into a path to paradise.

14. The material world provides endless means of salvation, of attaining God. But such means are open only to the disinterested. For those who seek gain, the world is nothing but a net and a fatal snare.

15. Property based upon love of God and a free heart is blessed. Property that is a *gift* brings a blessing with it. *Usurped* property brings down a curse. Possession may be avaricious or disinterested; avaricious possession is selfish, and disinterested — *eucharistic*. True human possession is to be found only in eucharistic property which comes from God and goes back to God through man. Only this spiritually-light possession which does not weigh down the spirit, does not nail us to temporal life or attract us to sin, can be called 'blessed.' It truly is blessed, whatever form it may take — possession of talents, gifts, things, lands, other people. All this is blessed — when it is in God. And all this is accursed when it separates us from God and makes the world into a god.

16. Eucharistic possession means everything for which people can *thank* God — and those through whom God gives it. Such gratitude implies both faith in God and the recognition that He is the Master of life. Through gratitude for life and for everything — the highest and most perfect expression of which is the *Eucharist* — man ascends to a new life, to the Kingdom of God. The infinitely small values of this world, salted with gratitude to God, become man's eucharistic property and remain 'his' forever as something new and great, transferred beyond the portals of eternity.

17. Property is a *conductor of love,* Divine and human. But men often make it a conductor of hatred for God and man. It is not property that is at fault, not the fact of possession, but *evil* possession or evil desire for possession.

18. Man is called to subdue the earth (GEN. 1, 28), and it is his privilege to *inherit* the earth (MATT. 5, 5).

3

The Second Birth

"... thou hearest the sound thereof, but canst not tell whence it cometh, and whither it goeth: so is every one that is born of the spirit" (John 3, 8).

BIRTH INTO THE HIGHER LIFE is a process as mysterious and in the last resort as incomprehensible as the growth of the child in the mother's womb. *There are visible signs of the conception and ripening of the earthly life,* and there are visible signs of the spiritual ripening and birth into the spirit of Christ. These signs do not rob us of mystery which surrounds all God's work in the world. But it is given to us to see that everything sinful becomes painful, difficult, repulsive; a man begins to find less and less pleasure in sin, and more and more pain and misery in it (while one who is spiritually dying, on the contrary, begins to find righteousness and purity more and more 'cramping,' and to get 'rest' and pleasure from sin). There is an awakening of that which is called 'conscience,' sensitiveness to good and evil. A man finds more and more weaknesses, failings and shortcomings in himself and is increasingly more eager to overcome them. At the same time he begins to understand that alone he is powerless in the struggle with sin and evil both in himself and in the surrounding world. And he begins to pray to God, knowing why he is praying, putting definite spiritual tasks before himself and asking from above for the gift of prayer and all the things mentioned by St. Paul in the Epistle to Galatians as the fruit of the Spirit (5, 22-26). The process of birth is connected with suffering. As the spiritual father "travails in birth" (GAL. 4, 19) until his son in Christ is born, so the newly-born suffers too as he begins to understand that all is not well with the world and to be conscious of its cold and alien forces and his own helplessness. Often a man's spiritual awakening is connected with external as well as with inner suffering (persecution for righteousness' sake).

It is a mistake to believe, as some people do, that "birth in spirit" can happen *at once*, as with St. Paul on the way to Damascus. St. Paul was not spiritually born on the way to Damascus (he had been a righteous and zealously believing Jew before then) — but it was as though a bandage fell off his eyes, and the whole power of his faith was turned to serving Him Whom he had persecuted 'in God's name.' No doubt St. Paul had been *inwardly prepared for that which happened on the way to Damascus by the whole of his preceding life;* and to the end of his days he disciplined himself, saying, "I keep under my body, and bring it into subjection" (I COR. 9, 27) and, "Brethren, I count not myself to have apprehended: but this one thing I do, forgetting those things which are behind, and reaching forth unto those things which are before, I press toward the mark for the prize of the high calling of God in Christ Jesus" (PHIL. 3, 13-14). "Let us therefore," he adds, *"as many as be perfect, be thus minded."*

This is an indication of the way toward 'birth from above' which St. Paul himself thought he had not yet attained. It is an example to all Christians. That is why men 'born in Christ' differ from others, not by apparent, but by the true humility. They do not regard themselves as having 'attained' anything; they see their deficiency in everything; they do not notice other people's failings, but on the contrary, are always struck by their good qualities.

Unfortunately, many people who sincerely seek the Lord are *deluded* by the thought that they have been 'born of the Spirit.' A man may experience spiritual joy, feel the warmth of prayer, find his Lord and Saviour and decide in his mind that this is 'second birth.' And indeed not infrequently he changes his conduct: gives up telling deliberate lies, drinking and smoking, begins to say his prayers, to read the Gospel daily—and in all sincerity numbers himself among the 'saved' and 'the risen in Christ.' In doing so he imperceptibly grows placid and satisfied with himself and his conduct, and then begins to look around and see who is 'saved' and who is 'not saved.' He goes to hear only such preachers who confirm his belief and, by specially selected texts from the Gospel, he is lulled to sleep in his spiritual complacency, thus barring the way to *poverty in spirit*, i.e. to true regeneration in Christ. The result is the type of the 'proud evangelical saint.' This is New Testament Pharisaism: "I am not like other men..." (in the parable of the publican and the Pharisee).

This false "birth" which deludes a good many of the 'righteous' opens the broad way to spiritual self-satisfaction and prevents a true 'birth in Christ,' i.e. the acceptance of the narrow and thorny way of spiritual poverty. But that was the way trodden by all the righteous, beginning with the Apostles, and they bequeathed it to us, their brethren. The nearer a man is to a mountain, the bigger it seems to him and the smaller he himself becomes in his own eyes. The nearer to the Lord, the smaller and more sinful he feels, and sincerely says, "I believe, Lord, and I acknowledge that Thou art of a truth the Christ, the Son of the living God, Which came into the world to save sinners, *of whom I am chief. . . ."* If one has that feeling, it is difficult to grow proud and regard oneself as 'saved' and another man as 'not saved.'

It is by God's great mercy that everyone who *truly believes* in the Son of God, the Lord Jesus Christ, 'has passed from death unto life' and is saved in his *true hope* that Christ's righteousness covers his unrighteousness; he becomes a redeemed child of God in Christ. But thou shouldst not forget, O man, that thou are not as yet in the world of 'vision' but in the world of *faith and hope.* Thou hast hope in Christ alone. Yes, it is a great hope that inspires thee, but it is *hope,* it is faith, and not vision. Remember the words: "thou standest by faith. Be not high-minded, but fear" (ROM. 11, 20).

It is a great Divine blessing that the Lord has hidden His judgment from us. We see the outer, and God sees the inner in each one of us. This is why it is such a sin to condemn others; this is why it is a sign of spiritual insensibility to disparage other people and extol oneself; and it is the height of insensibility to do so on the strength of God's word. The whole of the Gospel teaching rests on *the spirit of poverty.* Almighty God Himself gave up the wealth of His glory in order that we, fallen men, should feel poor in everything—poor in Christ. The more we love the Son of God Who was crucified for us and Who has redeemed us from eternal death, the more humble and poor in spirit we ought to be. A man who has *belittled himself in Christ* does not judge others and extol himself and, indeed, regards this as the greatest treachery to Christ to Whom alone all honour and all judgment belong. To Him belongs the honour of all our virtues, good actions, thoughts and feelings. "Every good gift and every perfect gift is from above, and cometh down from the Father of lights, with whom is no variableness, neither shadow of turning" (JAMES 1, 17). Every good that we have done is a *gift to us*—from God. This is why the righteous never accept for themselves the gratitude for the good given them to do out of love for God or man, but refer it to God.

These are the signs of true 'birth in Christ.' A man may be born in Christ before he is conscious of it. In the domain of consciousness there is control of heart and mind. But heart and mind may live a good life without being conscious of it. Indeed it is better that a good life should be lived unconsciously and that 'the right hand,' the mind, should not know what 'the left hand,' the heart does, and *vice versa*. It is better that man should forget about his good deeds, thoughts and feelings and should not even suspect their existence, *directing all his attention to the struggle against evil promptings of his heart and mind.*

At the Last Judgment the good will ask the Lord: "Lord, when saw we Thee an hungred, and fed Thee? or thirsty, and gave Thee drink? When saw we Thee a stranger, and took Thee in? or naked, and clothed Thee? Or when saw we Thee sick, or in prison, and came unto Thee?" (MATT. 25, 37-39). All these questions are *perplexities of righteousness*. Righteousness does not see its own worth; it sees only God's Righteousness and its own delinquency.

And, on the contrary, the sinners who answer the Lord with the same perplexity as the righteous have quite a different spirit: not the spirit of self-condemnation but of self-justification. They had never seen their evil, but only their (imaginary) good. They were proud; they were deluded and looked down upon others. But the righ-

116

teous belittled themselves before God and men. This is why they will receive God's unexpected verdict in a different way, just as they had lived differently. The righteous will marvel at their righteousness, and the sinners will be very much surprised at their sinfulness. Sinfulness will be a surprise to those who were never surprised at it on earth; righteousness will be a surprise to those who did not marvel at it on earth and did not even know that it was theirs.